THE DARK SIDE
OF THE SOUL

THE DARK SIDE OF THE SOUL

An Insider's Guide to the Web of Sin

STEPHEN CHERRY

BLOOMSBURY

LONDON · OXFORD · NEW YORK · NEW DELHI · SYDNEY

Bloomsbury Continuum
An imprint of Bloomsbury Publishing Plc

50 Bedford Square
London
WC1B 3DP
UK

1385 Broadway
New York
NY 10018
USA

www.bloomsbury.com

Bloomsbury, Continuum and the Diana logo are trademarks of
Bloomsbury Publishing Plc

First published 2016

British Library Cataloguing-in-Publication Data
A catalogue record for this book is available from the British Library.

Library of Congress Cataloguing-in-Publication data has been applied for.

ISBN: PB: 9781472900814
ePDF: 9781472900838
ePub: 9781472900821

2 4 6 8 10 9 7 5 3 1

Typeset by Integra Software Services Pvt. Ltd.
Printed and bound in Great Britain by CPI Group (UK) Ltd, Croydon CR0 4YY

To find out more about our authors and books visit www.bloomsbury.com.
Here you will find extracts, author interviews, details of forthcoming events and
the option to sign up for our newsletters.

To John Drury

You want to know God? First know yourself.

Evagrius Pontus c.345–399

CONTENTS

AUTHOR'S NOTE

In order to help make this book widely accessible I have not cluttered the pages with footnotes or references. However, the interested reader can find bibliographical and other material at the end of the book, from page 241.

Prologue:
The Viciousness of Vice

This book explores the dark side of the soul at a time when the word 'me' has never had it so good, but the word 'sin' has never had it so bad.

Ever since the Reformation sidelined the colourful idea of seven deadly sins, and replaced this extraordinarily fruitful invitation to the imagination with the Ten Commandments, interest in sin, so to speak, has been on the wane. Meanwhile, fascination with our own inner workings, our spirituality and our emotional wellbeing, has risen inexorably.

So perhaps it is time to connect our interest in our selves with the language of sin and vice, and see what wisdom might result.

While not aiming to reinstate the seven deadly sins in their traditional form, this book explores the sins and vices that are both intrinsic to who we are, and yet also apt to be the cause of our undoing and unhappiness. Our focus here is on the 'deadlies', or if you prefer, on our demons: naming them, exploring the relationships between them, and making some suggestions to help limit their power over us and the damage they can cause.

The trouble with sins and vices is not that they are desires that make us feel guilty or ashamed, or that they are forbidden behaviours. What makes sins and vices toxic is that when indulged in, pursued and explored they open up unimagined trajectories of harm and hurt and diminishment. As one of our wise guides to this territory, the philosopher Gabriele Taylor, has put it, the deadliness of the vices consists in 'the harm done to the self'. This is what makes the vices 'vicious'. It's that they are attitudes and behaviours by which the self is damaged, wounded, diminished, distorted and, if not destroyed, then isolated.

That's not the whole story, of course. Concern with vice and sin must be more than solipsistic. It's not *just* the self that suffers. It's others too, and a concern about sin and vice is as much about the common good as it is about individual flourishing. Indeed, the two have to go hand in hand. A scholarly book that reviews the tension between individual sin and social sin from the mid-nineteenth century to the era of liberation theologies comes to the conclusion that this dichotomy needs to be reconciled by thinking in terms of the *relational self*.

The point is well made. Self and society are not two separate spheres; both are products of relationship. Sins and vices are therefore fundamentally and ineluctably relational. That some of them are more internal, reflexive and self-regarding doesn't detract from the reality that their impact is equally experienced by family and friends, or that they survive and prosper not only in the soul but in the community and in society itself. Who we are, what we do, the nature of our inner dispositions and tendencies, and our accumulated habits, are rarely the result of our own bold and heroic self-determination. They are complex products of time and place, socialization and genetic predisposition, formal belief and ongoing reflection on experience. Trying to get behind all the external influences to the pristine and innocent, genuine, real and singular *me* is futile. We are always who we are in response to, and in relationship with, others.

The word 'me' may never have had it so good, but neither has the word 'relationship' or 'relational' or that sad word that speaks of our longing for a more nourishing connection with others – 'loneliness'. The experience of loneliness reminds us that we are social and relational to the core; the lonely heart is always a heart seeking fulfilment in the give and take of relationship.

And it is the hidden power, the hidden project if you will, of the sins and vices to make us deeply lonely. To cut us off from the relationships that can bring us to fulfilment.

Not that they present themselves in this way. Sins and vices are rarely self-evident, especially when they are our own sins and vices. They are often self-disguising; sometimes they even disguise themselves as virtues. Even when they come to our attention they can encourage self-deception and, when that fails, self-excuse. They are also insidious, and typically insinuate themselves into who we are before we properly realize the negative consequences of accommodating them. They lure us into thinking that although we know that we do have our faults, they are not really so very serious. But as Chaucer has the parson preach in the *Canterbury Tales*, 'Often and often I counsel that no man trust in his own perfection, save he be stronger than Samson, and holier than David and wiser than Solomon.'

Learning about the dark side of the soul is learning about yourself, and to learn about sin and vice is to grow in self-awareness that is sometimes painful. We can never know everything about the dark side of our soul, but we can become more alert to the negative side of who we are, even of those aspects of who we are that we sometimes fail to notice, sometimes deny and sometimes hate.

The point of seeking this difficult and always partial self-awareness is not simply to impress ourselves with our own wisdom. Indeed, if that is the aim we are sure to be defeated because when we become aware of the dark side of ourselves we learn things that by no means flatter us, and which we might prefer not to know. If more self-approval is your aim then you should read another book – there are plenty on the market. But if honest self-awareness in the interests of taking responsibility for, and nourishing, your relational self is what you have in mind, then the following pages are intended for you. Whatever your beliefs or mindset, you may find something that resonates truthfully, informs your introspection and self-observation, and offers a way forward – even if it sometimes involves a little squirming.

1

The Dark Side
of the Soul

Studying Sin

Imagine you hear that a new department is being created at a major
university. It is the department of Sin Studies. You are intrigued and
look up the details on the university's website, not realizing the date –
April 1st: April Fools' Day. This is what you read.

The University of Newchester is proud to announce that it has
received a multi-million-pound donation to establish the world's
first department of 'Sin Studies'. The department will have a
number of academic posts and run degree programmes at Bachelor,
Masters and PhD level. A committee is being established to appoint
the first Head of Department who is expected to be a leading
world expert on sin. Her or his first task will be to find the five
post-doctoral Research Fellows, junior academics able to devote
themselves exclusively to sin for a full three years. Undergraduates
will be admitted on to degree programmes in two years' time. The

programme is expected to be popular and to appeal particularly to the very many young people who have a keen interest in every aspect of sinning.

Full details of all the academic posts to be created await the arrival of the first Head of Department but the University is able to announce that there is a very generously endowed chair for the Professor of Greed, and an especially large one for the Professor of Gluttony. The Vice-Chancellor, Professor Screwtape, has said that he hopes that the Department will become the envy of several other universities and source of huge pride to Newchester.

You go on to read that although the professor was aware that the funding had come from a consortium of alumni with a known background in organized crime and narcotics trafficking, he had overridden the ethics committee and decided to accept the donation because it is only by studying sin directly that one can hope to understand its impact on humanity. He also commented on the rumour that he himself had received personal gifts from members of the consortium adding up to over a million pounds' worth of goods and benefits in recent years, saying that a number of them were good personal friends, but that this had no bearing on the decision either to establish the department or to award a number of the donors honorary degrees in recognition of their philanthropy. Very similar things had happened when the university opened its 'Happiness Department', with associated restaurant and spa, a few years earlier, a development which, he accepted, had yet to prove that it could raise the ambient level of happiness across the university. He explained that in both cases the hope was always to encourage other potential donors to follow the example of these generous people, and to show how even the most ill-gotten of gains could be put to a good purpose, whether making happiness or understanding sins and vices.

It is of course impossible to imagine a Vice-Chancellor of any real university making such a speech. Structures of governance, and operational checks and balances, compliance procedures and professional protocols are put in place precisely to prevent this sort of thing happening. The more time goes by, the more codes of compliance and practices of due-diligence dominate the minds of those in positions of corporate leadership and responsibility, and thereby ensure that the highest standards of probity are maintained. Or so we hope.

But the greater point of this imaginative exercise is to underline the extreme unlikelihood that 'sin' might be considered a sensible area for any kind of intellectual investigation or research. Why is this? Why might we suppose that the study of sin is unlikely to reveal anything surprising or significant? Surely any reading of the daily news, coupled with even the lightest monitoring of the increase in bureaucratic and juridical effort required to cope with the aftermath of felony and wickedness, is enough to suggest that there is such a reality as 'sin' and that it would be as well to be informed and wise about it. The notion that investigating sin might yield something worthwhile is not, when you think about it, entirely counter-intuitive. Indeed, in the long run it could even prove to be cost-effective.

But we do need to clear some hurdles before we can take sin seriously. As theologian Alistair McFadyen has put it, there is a 'now-conventional association . . . between the language of sin and what are seen to be trivial (though often as titillating) peccadilloes and temptations'. As he rightly adduces, 'such trivialization itself reflects the fact that the language of "sin" has fallen largely into disuse in general public (but also in much Christian and theological) discourse as a language for talking about the pathological in human affairs'. McFadyen suggests three reasons why this may be so: the general secularization of our culture, the fear that the Christian understanding of sin is neither moral nor scientific, and the suspicion that 'sin is a language of blame and condemnation', used in religious enclaves to whip up guilt and shame. Sin is a dodgy word today, and much mocked. As Francis Spufford put it, 'Everybody knows . . . that "sin" basically means "indulgence" or "enjoyable naughtiness"'.

The Bible, on the other hand, says that 'the wages of sin is death'. That is something to be considered at a more advanced level of the curriculum of Sin Studies, perhaps, but the notion that sin is expensive, both for the individual sinner and for the wider society, is plausible. It's not just that it costs in the order of £36,000 per year to keep a person in prison (just imagine if that same person had that amount spent on their education), or that gluttony puts pounds both on your grocery bill and on your weight, or that avarice is the distortion of financial thinking and desire which makes the rich feel poor, and thereby motivates them to acquire in such a way as to keep the poor really poor. Sin is expensive in many ways, as any serious study of the subject will inevitably expose.

The Newchester announcement is arguably quite correct in asserting that 'Sin Studies' is likely to be a popular subject, because, obviously, sin absolutely fascinates us. Stroll into any bookshop and see the amount of space given over to crime or even 'true crime'. Think of the detective stories that are popular in short-story or television programme format. Think of what you think and worry about. Think about what people discuss. If someone begins to tell you what a colleague or neighbour has done 'now', you can be fairly sure that you are not going to hear a story that highlights their merits or virtues.

Human beings are fascinated by sin and vice. The interest is definitely there and the consequences are huge, but 'sin' has developed a very bad name for itself over the last few centuries and, for a whole variety of reasons, has ceased to be a piece of helpful vocabulary for those who seek to understand the human condition in general, and themselves in particular. But might it just be that by declining to think in terms of ourselves as sinners, or as people who have vices that we vaguely know about and generally regret but prefer not to name or deal with, we are colluding with evil itself? Because whatever we think of notions like sin and vice today, we have never been better informed about the prevalence of evil in the world.

Naming Evil

Although today the word 'sin' has almost passed from public discussion, except in cases where people are discussing self-indulgent pleasures that might be frowned upon by those of an especially religious or pleasure-hating disposition, the word 'evil' is called upon regularly when people are shocked by an atrocity which seems to have the marks of callous calculation. When two policewomen, Nicola Hughes and Fiona Bone, were killed in cold blood in Manchester in September 2012, the Prime Minister, David Cameron, said that it was 'an act of shocking evil by an appalling individual'. The remark was widely judged to have been appropriate. Had he used the occasion to talk about sin he would certainly not have caught the public mood. And rightly not – the words have different meanings, but in recent years the use of 'evil' has expanded while the use of 'sin' has declined, and this warrants some reflection before we look in detail at the dark side of the soul. It is important, after all, given that there is to be introspection here, to know whether or not we might find evil in our own semi-darkness or whether we can be guaranteed, as we set out, to find that we are, as we hope we might be, generally well-intentioned people who occasionally make the sort of mistakes that are easily excused; except on those rare occasions when we do something that we are deeply ashamed of, or neglect to do something that we subsequently really wish we had, in which case we fall into a state of self-appalled-ness and say, 'the trouble is that I can't forgive myself'.

When people reach for the word 'evil' it's often not clear whether the speaker is saying that the act is evil or that the perpetrator of the act is an evil person. Moreover, it is by no means apparent what exactly the word 'evil' is intended to mean in such situations, beyond the notion that 'any decent person would be outraged and disgusted'. Nonetheless, when people today use the word 'evil' you can be sure that they are intending to be taken very seriously, and that they expect those who hear them to nod in agreement. Evil is not up for negotiation, even in an educated liberal democracy. It is a word that comes from deep within us, indicating that our ethical judgement has come from our guts. We reach for the word 'evil' when what we observe evokes in us moral disgust. It has become the go-to word when we need to add ethical gravitas and shocked indignation to our disappointment with others.

But people don't use the word 'evil' simply to add ethical and emotional colour. There is cognitive content too. 'Evil' means something like, 'behaviour that is extraordinary, and cannot and should not be dealt with in the language normally used to describe the ways in which decent human beings conduct their affairs'. It also suggests that the state of mind, the motivation, the degree of cruelty and callousness of the perpetrator is beyond the furthest reaches of our capacity for empathy. Evil implies that both the act and the motivation are so negatively exceptional as to be off the scale. Use of the word is therefore defensive and distancing. It is a way of making the point that the person who disgusts us is fundamentally alien to us. In this way the idea of 'evil' is connected to the idea of 'monster'. To be 'evil' is be unforgivable, beyond redemption, but almost more importantly in the public mind, to be beyond the bounds of normal, decent, healthy society. To be evil is to have stepped beyond, or to have been exposed as being, way beyond the pale of unconditional positive regard, or the reach of empathy.

The defensive dynamics of the use of the word 'evil' are subtle and complex. For instance, the failure in empathy of the person who calls another 'evil' is not understood as a matter of personal failure by that person, but to be indicative of a fact about the other. Those who see perpetrators as evil monsters are creating a thick cocoon of spiritual isolation for themselves and those with whom they find it easy and pleasant to identify. The attractions of this are manifest. It is deeply troubling, when we hear of an act of cruelty, or of the abuse of power, or of premeditated violence, to think that I, myself, might have been responsible. It is far easier to identify with the victim, than to imagine that I might have been the perpetrator. And while we might

often fear that we ourselves, or one of our loved ones, might one day
fall victim to a person of evil intent, we don't normally stretch our
minds to imagine that those who perpetrate acts of malevolent harm
might also fear being hurt, and in all probability have themselves
been hurt. Thus we fail to see a world of hurt or damaged people
who go on to inflict more harm on others than they ever imagine
or intend, and instead divide the world into two groups of people.
The first group is 'most of us' who are, on the whole, good. We are
normal people who, despite our slips and gaffes and errors, remain
fundamentally decent. When we fail we need to be understood,
excused or forgiven – probably by ourselves as much as by anyone
else – for letting ourselves down. Then there are people who are quite
different to us, and so need to be regarded and treated exceptionally.
The circle whereby the evil are identified, isolated, alienated and
deemed to be absolutely different to us – the likes of you and me – is
thus complete.

The point of this brief excursus into the defensive language of
'evil' is that the much less attractive language of sin or vice does
not encourage this kind of thinking. The point about sin is that 'all
have sinned'. The category of 'sinners' is not a subset of humanity,
but the whole of humanity. This point is repeatedly lost and the
language of sin itself abused in creating just the exclusionary
dynamics that I have described above. However, it is a significant
part of the argument of this book that the language of sin, when
richly understood and properly used, creates a dynamic which
is precisely the reverse of the defensive one described here, and
thereby opens the door to what one might call the 'spirituality of
enlarged compassion and endless empathy'. To put it another way,

what the language of sin offers us is a way of naming what is wrong without pretending that doing wrong is an extreme aspect of a few characters. Rather, to talk of sins and vices is to see the origins of evil not in the pernicious eccentricities of the few, but in common aspects of the human nature that we all share.

As a Bee Produces Honey

In a lecture in 1961, William Golding, the schoolmaster turned author who wrote *Lord of the Flies* – a novel that was on the syllabus for high school exams for decades in Great Britain, and which he described as a 'fable' – indicated that the Second World War had had a huge impact on his beliefs. His biographer John Carey explains.

> He [Golding] . . . used to believe, before the war, in the perfect-ibility of social man – that all social ills could be removed by reorganizing society . . . However, the Second World War and its atrocities destroyed that trust, and he came to see that 'man produces evil as a bee produces honey'. He wrote *Lord of the Flies* out of a belief in original sin, derived not from books but from watching how people behave.

After the Second World War, the Nuremberg war trials led to the execution of many leading Nazis. Looking back with hindsight, it is hard to avoid the sense that this was a purge; that it was not only appropriate retribution for large-scale murder and crimes against humanity, but that it was also a way of excising from the human community its most evil members, a way of cleaning up the human family. In fact such a view always seems to lie somewhere behind the use of the death penalty, however else it is argued out. The justification given is that some people really are too far gone, too exceptional in their evil, to be accommodated by society – even in prison.

A few decades after the war, however, a number of psychological studies suggested that contrary to the way in which people like to think of themselves, it's not just the evil few who might, in the right (that is, very wrong) circumstances end up obeying malicious and malevolent instructions and inflict wanton cruelty on others, but the many. Psychological experiments suggested that one could quite easily create circumstances in which a random collection of young men will start acting out barbaric roles, or in which ordinary people will inflict serious electric shocks on other ordinary people who happen to fail a simple laboratory test. When these scientific studies by Philip Zimbardo and Stanley Milgram were coupled with the publication in 1963 of Hannah Arendt's *Eichmann in Jerusalem: A Report on the Banality of Evil*, people began to wake up to the truth that the world isn't populated by mainly good people and messed up by a few extraordinarily bad people. The penny was dropping that the truth about evil is much more unsettling than we had thought, and that the origins of human-caused suffering lie much closer to home. It's not that there are just a few bad apples; it's that all the apples are potentially very bad. 'As for me,' people began to realize, 'well, I'm an apple too.' Speaking theologically for a moment, we are in the territory of original sin.

The biblical roots of the idea of original sin lie in St Paul who, in one of his more honest and self-aware moments, observed that, whatever his best intentions, he would all too often let himself down.

Paul's famous meditation on this is in the letter to the Romans, in which he attributes his inability to do the good that he wills to 'the flesh'. Let me rephrase his words to attribute this negativity not to the flesh, but to the dark side of the soul. My words are in italics.

> For we know that the law is spiritual; *but I know that I am only partly aware of the workings of my own mind, and that sin and vice inhabit the dark side of my soul*. I do not understand my own actions. For I do not do what I want, but I do the very thing I hate. Now if I do what I do not want, I agree that the law is good. But in fact it is no longer I that do it, but sin *and vice* that dwell within me, *hidden on the dark side*. For I know that nothing good dwells within me, that is, *in the darker reaches of my soul*. I can will what is right, but I cannot do it. For I do not do the good I want, but the evil I do not want is what I do. Now if I do what I do not want, it is no longer I that do it, but sin that dwells within me, *hidden beneath my awareness and beyond my control*.
>
> So I find it to be a law that when I want to do what is good, evil lies close at hand. For I delight in the law of God in the *bright inner me that I most love*, but I see in my *soul* another law at war with the law of my *enlightened* mind, making me *captive within the web of sin that stretches across the dark side of my soul*. Wretched *person* that I am! Who will rescue me from this *relentless inner tangle*?

Paul's passage is part of his argument about the need for an act of salvation that is outside ourselves. The psychology of it has rightly been criticized as dualistic, attributing what is wrong with us as a whole to our bodies. There is a strong tradition of this in Christianity, and despite the fact that the Gnostics – for whom this body–mind split was essential and whose thinking was relentlessly dualistic – have repeatedly been denounced as heretics, it has proved to be remarkably persistent.

One of the truths that the puzzling notion of original sin is intended to illuminate is that there is no way back to a state of pure innocence in the history of humanity. What happened before that, while humanity was yet innocent, is a matter of speculation. In that way it is like the question of what happened before the 'big bang' that sparked the material universe. The difference between theologians and cosmologists, however, is that while cosmologists often shrug their shoulders and say, maybe with a frown, 'that's not a proper question', theologians have been inclined to go along with, and interpret, the human desire for myth and explanation that gives some kind of shape to the unknowable. And so we have the story of Adam and Eve, and all the weight that is put upon it, when it comes to the origins of sin.

There's a place for the imagination of religion and the modesty of science in any culture, and the questions of where sin comes from, and why, and how life would be if it were not for sin and vice, have all occupied many great minds in the past, and still trouble some people today. But they are not the focus here. And so we give the question of the *origins* of sin the shoulder-shrug approach, and we take the 'fallen-ness', the imperfection and the imperfectibility of human beings as a given. Our question is not, how does it happen that human beings have a dark side? Or even, do all human beings have a dark side to their soul? But rather, what can we learn about the dark side of our own soul, given that we will never understand it fully? And how can we live with it, given that we will never completely control it?

Murky Border Country

In a witty and amusing book called *The Joy of Sin*, Simon Laham takes an evolutionary psychological approach to the traditional seven deadly sins and shows how they are all part of our natural and necessary functioning. He argues that, without appetite for food and sex, for instance – that is, gluttony and lust – we would soon come to an end as a species. Our economy is necessarily based on greed and envy; we all need to have rest, sleep and relaxation, so sloth too plays a part; and without a sense of pride we lack self-esteem and never get very much done at all. Spritely and provocative as Laham's approach to the seven deadly sins is, and helpful as a critique of the negative, simplistic, judgement-generating and prejudice-inspiring teaching about sins that has been, and is, all too common, it is not as radical as it may at first seem. Dig back to the origins of thinking about sins and vices and you find that they were understood in the first place not as corruptions that would lead to damnation, but as ways of *thinking* that were both necessary and intrinsically dangerous. Originally analysed and listed not to divide the world into the sinners and the righteous, but as a kind of self-help for those whose minds and hearts wandered in the direction of unhappiness and dis-ease, they are perhaps better described as *hostile pleasures*, or *potentially problematic passions*. They are necessary, but they often go wrong. They are not the perversions of the few but constitute part of the intellectual, emotional and spiritual makeup of us all.

The difficulty for us with sins and vices, the hostile pleasures and potentially problematic passions, is not that they are the clear marks of the corrupt nature of the perverse. It is that they are complex and subtle and self-damaging as well as other-damaging aspects of our necessary makeup. Moreover they are not manifest and clear to us. That is why the metaphor of the 'dark side of the soul' is apt for describing them together, and why a guide to introspection is called for. Despite the fact that such a book as this is inevitably written, at least some of the time, in the third person, and while we cannot but help think of the sins, failings, flaws and vices of others, the primary purpose of thinking about sins and vices is neither to stack up guilt for ourselves, nor to enable us better to judge and blame others. The point and purpose of thinking about sin and vice is to help us develop a realistic, helpful and healthy self-understanding as a relational and responsible self.

If this were easy, this book would serve no purpose – and sin wouldn't be half what it's cracked up to be; nor would the world be in the pickle it has been in since human beings became, through consciousness and collaboration, an unrivalled power among the animal species of this world. But sin and vice are important parts of who we are, even if we are only vaguely aware of them, lurking, as they do, in the shadowy side of our self. We won't capture them easily or completely, and will need all our powers of both analysis and metaphor to understand them slightly better.

Sins and vices subsist in the murky border country of our minds. It is a land of rolling mists and quicksands, of slippery slopes and long winding paths that prove to be dead ends; it's a country of clear signage announcing 'come this way' that leads to a lethal precipice;

a place of rewards that turn into punishments, of hopes that prove to be vain, and promises that turn to ashes in our hands. This is the dark side of the soul. It is not pitch black, but neither is it ever transparent or straightforward. And it is dark in more than one way. First, because it's rarely possible to work out what's really going on in there. In what follows I have tried to be as clear and plain as I can, but the task of illuminating this has often felt like lighting a small match in a humidly steaming tropical rainforest. I say this not to malign rainforests but to offer an image of the density and complexity of this land of perpetual dusk. And second, it is dark in the sense that it isn't good. Some of the sins and vices have splendid PR officers, they scrub up very nicely when they go on display, and, like all of us, they try to put their best foot forward when they have the opportunity to make a first impression. But there is often something negative, destructive or malicious in the mix of what we think, say and do; in the reality of who we are. That's what we are on the lookout for here.

Reviewing what he learnt when, as a prisoner in the Gulag, he had endless time for introspection, Alexander Solzhenitsyn wrote,

Looking back, I saw that for my whole conscious life I had not understood either myself or my strivings. What had seemed for so long to be beneficial now turned out in actuality to be fatal, and I had been striving to go in the opposite direction to that which was truly necessary to me. But just as the waves of the sea knock the inexperienced swimmer off his feet and keep tossing him back onto the shore, so also was I painfully tossed back on dry land by the blows of misfortune. And it was only because of this that I was able to travel the path which I had always really wanted to travel.

It was granted me to carry away from my prison years on my bent back, which nearly broke beneath its load, this essential experience: *how* a human being becomes evil and *how* good. In the intoxication of youthful successes I had felt myself to be infallible, and I was therefore cruel. In the surfeit of power I was a murderer, and an oppressor. In my most evil moments I was convinced that I was doing good, and I was well supplied with systematic arguments. And it was only when I lay there rotting on prison straw that I sensed within myself the first stirrings of good. Gradually it was disclosed to me that the line separating good and evil passes not through states, nor between classes, nor between political parties either – but right through every human heart – and through all human hearts. This line shifts. Inside us, it oscillates with the years. And even within the hearts overwhelmed by evil, one small bridgehead of good is retained. And even in the best of all hearts, there remains . . . an un-uprooted small corner of evil.

Solzhenitsyn's 'un-uprooted small corner of evil' is hidden deep within the dark side of the soul. His insight that the line separating good from evil passes through every human heart reflects another line from Paul's letter to the Romans, 'all have sinned, and all have fallen short of the glory of God.'

The tradition of which the seven deadly sins are a part reflects on the worst things that human beings think, feel and behave – not least towards each other. This model and approach requires us to believe not that most of us (including me) are good and some others very bad, or that what matters most about us is the degree of our badness, or that in some cases the word 'bad' is an understatement and that only 'evil' will do, but that all have sinned (including me), and that there is a perspective, call it divine, enlightened or worldly-wise, which recognizes that a hair's breadth separates the best of us from the worst of us, and that it therefore ill-behoves us to focus on the shortcomings of others. As Jesus taught, 'Judge not and ye shall not be judged' and, more metaphorically, 'Why do you see the speck in your neighbour's eye, but do not notice the log in your own eye? Or how can you say to your neighbour, "Friend, let me take out the speck in your eye", when you yourself do not see the log in your own eye? You hypocrite, first take the log out of your own eye, and then you will see clearly to take the speck out of your neighbour's eye.' To adapt the metaphor to fit better with our theme we might say, 'it's not appropriate to speculate about the malice and malignancy inside others while neglecting to acknowledge, explore and seek to illuminate the dark side of your own soul'.

The truth of the matter is probably that once we have at least a little insight into the dark side of our own soul, once we have some sense of the sins and vices that lurk there, we will be less inclined to imagine that there are monsters of purely evil intent lurking around the place. This sense of solidarity in sin and vice, sad though it is, is both healthy and humanizing, and the basis of a realistic sense of community – whether that community is a nuclear family, a rural settlement, an international institution, a metropolitan city or a nation-state. This 'solidarity in sin' implies that we are all more or less motivated by, and subject to, forces and influences that are within us and yet about which we have less awareness than we routinely suppose, and that some of these, at least some of the time, are problematic, if not toxic, or hostile. And here's the rub. These are all aspects of who we are, and therefore, whether or not we keep this stuff under cover of darkness, it remains our responsibility.

2

The Deadlies

The tradition in which this exploration finds itself has its origins in the hermit Evagrius of Pontus who in the fourth century outlined what he believed to be the most dangerous 'passions'. He didn't call them sins. The word he used was *logismoi*, which might just as correctly be translated 'thoughts' or 'words'. His list was of eight and he was earnestly serious in his attempts to understand them and thereby limit their power.

Evagrius, as befits a man of his time, tended to think of these thoughts not only as 'passions' arising from the heart and mind, but also as demons that visited from outside. This threefold nature of a sin or vice (that it is experienced as thought, passion and demon) suggests that there is often both a cognitive and an affective side to our vices, and an intuition that they don't have their origins precisely in us, but that they assail us from without. We need not believe in demons to honour this intuition. The point is *not* that our sins and vices, or the temptations to indulge and engage them, come from absolutely outside ourselves; it's that they come from the part of us where our self-awareness is minimal. That is, the murky and obscure side of who we are that we are calling the dark side of the soul, that place where the light of self-knowledge does not often shine, and where it never shines brightly. It's when we feel assailed by a demon that the dark side of our soul is making its presence felt.

A Little List

Evagrius' list of thoughts or passions was: gluttony, fornication, avarice, anger, sadness, acedia, vainglory and pride. These are clearly a strange mixture of the familiar and the surprising, but they are also, I suggest, a mixture of both the easily recognized and understood and the genuinely puzzling to us, so a word or two explaining each is in order.

It's odd that a hermit who ate just once a day put 'gluttony' at the top of the list. He didn't mean, and probably didn't imagine, the sort of behaviour that leads to cholesterol-filled arteries or that fuels the current obesity epidemic. He was talking about our attitude to food, more than our calorific intake. For Evagrius, gluttony was all about fussiness and wanting food to be more exciting than it is. This doesn't seem worth thinking about today, and like many things is a matter of context. Yet, while we are all increasingly fussy with our dietary preferences, fussiness about food is, historically at least, a strange priority, and in certain situations, such as war, a very unhelpful one, and Evagrius was in the desert living a hermit life in order to do spiritual battle, not to open a tea shop for tourists or to prepare to enter a cookery competition.

Unlike later lists of sins that talk about lust, Evagrius used a word that is normally translated 'fornication'. In the Greek in which he wrote, the word was *pornea* – from which we get our word 'pornography'. Living alone, he was much troubled by both the fantasy and the reality of women. Two background points are relevant here. In his pre-hermit career Evagrius had an affair with a married woman. A second point is that he felt that gluttony led on to fornication – especially if food was too moist or if too much water was drunk.

'Avarice' for Evagrius included both 'the love of money' and greed for items and objects, possessions as we now call them, more generally. Indeed, his view is that the demon that provokes avarice is 'the most varied and ingenious in deceit'. He would be critical not only of your shopping trolley and the size of removal van you need, but also of all the things you have owned for a while and then given and thrown away, not to mention your family photograph collections – seeing treasured memories as equally binding.

Context is important when it comes to understanding what Evagrius means by 'anger'. He is in the desert to contemplate and pray and yet he finds that anger is one of the worst inhibitors of the peacefulness that is needed for the spiritual life. He is not talking about the sort of anger that comes when we reflect on injustice; he's talking about bitter resentment, irritability, irascibility, and fantasies of acting out negative feelings towards others: interpersonal irritations that escalate and circle round in the mind.

'Sadness' is another of Evagrius' *logismoi*. It is often a consequence of frustrated anger but can also be prompted by nostalgia for the pleasures of a less arduous past. It leads, he believes, to inertia and apathy. In lists drawn up after the time of Evagrius, 'sadness' was replaced by envy. The reason for this is that the sadness here is caused by the pathetic and inevitably frustrated desire that things should be other than they are. As well as seeing sadness flowing from anger, Evagrius also sees that anger might be the result of sadness. The original vicious circle.

'Acedia' is the most obviously unfamiliar word on the list. For many years it was translated 'sloth' but these days scholars tend to leave it untranslated; I can see why and will follow that example. Acedia is a Greek word, and the original meaning is something like 'carelessness' or 'negligence'. In perhaps his most famous passage, Evagrius calls this the 'noonday demon'; referring not only to the lethargy that comes upon us when the sun gets to its zenith, but also back to a verse in Psalm 91: 'the destruction that wastes at noonday'. This evokes a feeling familiar to anyone who finds their energy sapping away mid-morning and not returning until late in the afternoon; 'restlessness' is the way one self-confessed victim of acedia has put it. Henry David Thoreau more romantically called it 'quiet despair'. Others more prosaically think of it as 'prevarication' whereas writers might equate it with their famous 'block'. Acedia is apathy and boredom that come and go, rather than congenitally low levels of energy. One scholarly article connects it with 'burnout syndrome' – the sense that, after all that effort that seemed to get me nowhere, I just can't be bothered any more. Its relationship both to trivial mood swings and to serious mental health issues make acedia especially tricky and particularly important to discuss today.

'Vainglory' is seventh on the list. No longer a word much used in everyday English, it is the desire for human esteem. You could do worse than to think of it as 'status anxiety'. Why is this so bad? Evagrius was very high-minded – what matters is what you think about, and how your thoughts move up the scale from contemplating material things to ideas to God. Thinking about what people think of you, and how they rank or esteem you, is basically not on his map of values – and yet, human beings being what they ever are, these are the sorts of thoughts that pop up and get in the way. Not only is this a contemplative problem, it can also be a practical problem, as vainglory can lead us on to harmful actions. In particular Evagrius, in a phrase that some think might have precise autobiographical reference, believes that it may well be the prelude to fornication – the temptation not being to the carnal pleasure itself but to the vainglorious delight of knowing that others know, or of enjoying your own reputation.

Finally we come to 'pride', which far from being the pleasant glow that comes after personal success is a product of a particular failure – the failure to give God the credit for all good works. Evagrius really doesn't like pride. In an aphorism he writes that pride is 'a tumour of the soul filled with pus; when it has ripened it will rupture and create a great disgusting mess'. In the tradition that evolved from Evagrius, pride became the fountain of all other sins and it is possible, I think, that for Evagrius pride was as close to the essence of sin as it was possible to get. To be proud in this sense is to have mistaken oneself for God. Evagrius espoused the 'contraries cure contraries' theory and so saw the antidote to pride in its opposite: humility. He commented that the word of a humble person is 'a soothing ointment for the soul'. He doesn't say what the word of a proud person is like, but we all know the rasping effect on the ears and the soul of those who think they are God.

Shawn Taylor offers a helpful comment on the way in which Evagrius' overall scheme serves the purpose of achieving the stillness, peace and imperturbability that are the precondition, the nature and the fruit of prayer:

The achievement works in logical progression. A monk – the audience Evagrius addresses – must learn the fundamental and practical skills. One must first recognize and overcome temptation of one's bodily passions, including gluttony, lust, and greed. In addition one must properly harness psychic or emotional states, overcoming sadness, anger and acedia with patience and courage. The rational faculty must also be properly yoked, eliminating vainglory and pride with prudence and humility.

From Thoughts to Vices

Evagrius was not a law maker but a pastor. His thinking was a very early form of psychology. He was concerned to enlighten his fellow monks about the demons that were assailing them and to advise them as best he could about how to respond to their distractions and temptations. He was concerned not to make rules and regulations about how people should live, but to help people with what he would have seen as the most important part of their lives – their spiritual battles. Pope Gregory realized that it was often too much to expect of a person that they fight with passions and vices that present themselves as powerful and cunning demons, and so he instituted the notion of seven deadly sins to facilitate external control.

Gregory's list is rather different to Evagrius'. In particular it begins with pride (into which he enfolds vainglory) and ends with gluttony. He also replaces fornication with lust, while introducing envy and removing sadness. His list is therefore, pride, envy, anger, acedia, avarice, lust and gluttony. It is more or less in the reverse order to

Evagrius' thoughts, reflecting what one writer has called a transition from a bubble-up theory of sin to a trickle-down version. In fact it might be better to suggest a contrast between an out-in and a top-down model of how it works.

The out-in theory that fits with Evagrius' view is based on the idea that we are basically sound and integral beings, capable of doing the right thing but from time to time assailed by demons who tempt us from outside ourselves.

The top-down theory of Gregory is that we are muddled and confused in our being – even at the level of our will – and for reasons we can't properly fathom, don't seem to be able to do right for doing wrong. Here Gregory is more in line with Augustine, who takes his cue both from personal experience and St Paul, in believing that there really is a deep-seated problem in us and that to deal with it we need to recognize our intrinsic distance from God. For theologians of this ilk, such honesty about ourselves and our limits is humility, and it is humility that makes us redeemable and drives the penitential aspects of spirituality – the desire to be forgiven and absolved for our faults and weaknesses, the 'manifold sins and wickedness' which those who pray using the Book of Common Prayer 'acknowledge and bewail'. Its opposite is pride, which is to believe, and to act on the belief, that I myself am not only a splendid and fine being as I am, but that I am every bit as good as God and, for all practical purposes, can take the place of God. This is the understanding of pride that makes it the fount of all other sins.

There are other differences too between Gregory's approach and Evagrius', and it should be noted that Gregory didn't get Evagrius straight from the horse's mouth but via another writer for monks – Cassian. When Thomas Aquinas writes about the deadly sins he follows the lead given by Gregory – except that he doesn't use the same order. The form in which the list of the deadly sins came to dominate the medieval religious imagination was organized not around any particular theory of sin or the idea that one sin was more important or generative than any other but by a mnemonic, 'SALIGIA'. If this is surprising to the reader, it is perhaps because it only works in Latin. This is how it goes: Superbia, Avaritia, Luxuria, Ira, Gula, Invidia, Acedia. In English that is: Pride, Avarice, Lust, Wrath, Gluttony, Envy, Sloth. When Dante describes purgatory in *The Divine Comedy* he uses a deliberately vertical system – with the worst sinners at the bottom nearer hell and the lesser ones at the top nearer heaven. Starting from the hell-end he has precipices on which are successively found the proud, the envious, the angry, the slothful, the avaricious, the gluttonous and the promiscuous. Thus, for Dante, pride is the worst and promiscuity the least severe of the sins needing purgation.

When surveying Christianity in the West in the three hundred years before, during and after the Reformation, the historian John Bossy says that the list was, 'pride, envy, anger, avarice, gluttony, sloth and lechery' – in that order. And he adds that, 'As a moral system the seven deadly sins were not a model of coherence, and expositors differed a good deal in their attempts to reduce them to order.' There is some understatement here – 'not a model of coherence' indeed. Bossy suggests that one of the things that happened through the Reformation is that the Ten Commandments came to replace the seven deadly sins as the normative moral framework. This is why it is lists of the Ten Commandments that are written up as murals or on tablets in English Parish churches, rather than depictions of the seven deadly sins that predominate in older literature or art.

The attempt to bring some kind of coherence to lists of sins in this tradition often involved distinguishing between those sins that were more to do with the flesh – these being less significant – and those of the spirit, which were more serious. Thus pride, envy and anger were seen as serious, spiritual, sins whereas gluttony, lechery and sloth were seen as less serious sins of the body. Not everyone agreed about where sloth should fit, and there was widespread ambiguity about where to locate avarice.

There has recently been some resurgence in the idea that the traditional list of seven deadly sins does adequately cover the territory of human negativity and naughtiness. A number of books have sought to breathe new life into the old bones, and the philosopher Gabriele Taylor has declared in her non-theological account that the seven deadly sins were 'correctly so named and correctly classed together'. Taylor calls them deadly vices and has on her list, sloth, envy, covetousness (which is her interpretation of *avaritia* – avarice), pride, anger, lust and gluttony. She also smuggles in a long reflection on self and self-consciousness, which she doesn't seem to count in her list despite the resemblance of self-consciousness to vainglory. A rather different view is taken by another philosopher, Judith Shklar, who turns her attention to what she calls 'ordinary vices'. Whereas deadly sins are offences against the divine order, ordinary vices are more like character flaws; the sort of everyday nastiness that we expect of each other. Her list derives from her hero Montaigne, who in his essay 'On Cannibals' wrote, 'treachery, disloyalty, cruelty, tyranny . . . are our ordinary vices'. But hers is a longer and slightly different list, headed by cruelty and incorporating hypocrisy, snobbery, betrayal and misanthropy.

Not Quite So Simple

Shklar believes that 'it is only if we step outside the divinely ruled moral universe that we can really put our minds to the common ills we inflict on one another every day', and there are plenty who would agree with her that to think in terms of sin, a distinctively religious word, is unhelpful. In *The Joy of Sin* Simon Laham offers a slightly different critique of this tradition when he asserts that, 'even the deadliest of vices can make you smart, successful and happy'. His book provides convincing evidence, he believes, that the traditional seven deadly sins (his list is: lust, gluttony, greed, sloth, anger, envy and pride) are in fact normal or good human dispositions. He believes that when we look at them from the perspective of contemporary psychology, traditional moral theology evaporates into the puff of unhelpful steam it always has been. The book concludes that

> seven psychological characteristics of the human species that have for about sixteen centuries been demonized as mortally sinful are in fact rather good for us. All it takes to get to this conclusion is a little careful thought, a perusal of the scientific record, and a willingness to abandon a cultural legacy that drastically simplifies human nature.

The author's last word is that the word 'sin' itself is useless. 'Almost any facet of human behaviour – from genetic engineering to selfishness – is too complex, too multifaceted, and in the end often simply too functional to be given the label "sin".'

There are several claims in this, of which the last one, that sin is 'functional', is perhaps the easiest to agree with. Thomas Aquinas took a similar view, and if anything has a more subtle understanding of human nature and behaviour than Laham evidences in his book. One might also add, as many of the early Christian writers believed, that the behaviours and character traits that we think of as sins or vices are also, at least in the first instance, or in moderate doses, *pleasurable*. As we have noted, they have been thought of as *hostile pleasures*. So yes, what we call sins and vices may well have a part to play in our healthy functioning, but they can also, as it were, turn on us, or suddenly trap us, or even begin to control us in ways that are not functional and which diminish or destroy our capacity to flourish.

It is also possible to find common cause with Laham when he asserts that human behaviour is too complex and multi-faceted to be adequately and comprehensively categorized by the vocabulary of sin. The following observations perhaps underline the point. Some imaginative readers of children's literature, and watchers of children's films, have noted from time to time that certain characters can be reasonably well described in terms of the deadly sins. Perhaps the most convincing example of this is Roald Dahl's *Charlie and the Chocolate Factory* in which it has been alleged that each of the principal characters illustrates one of the deadly sins:

Augustus Gloop – gluttony

Veruca Salt – greed

Violet Beauregarde – pride

Mike Teavee – sloth

Grandpa Joe – envy

Charlie – lust

Willy Wonka – wrath.

Readers who are familiar with this work may choose to think through how convincing this is. Other commentators have done a similar exercise with characters from A. A. Milne's *The House at Pooh Corner* and related stories. What is especially interesting about this is that there is by no means universal agreement about which character goes with which sin. Eeyore, for instance, is identified by some as the model of sloth, whereas others see him as primarily exhibiting envy. Some see Piglet as the envious one, whereas others feel Piglet to be consumed by greed on the grounds that he has an unnecessarily large house. But then there are those who see Rabbit as the epitome of greed or avarice, while others see her as wrathful. The lovable Tigger is meanwhile identified by some as being full of lust, whereas others, who notice that Tigger never tidies up, see Tigger as slothful. The only designations that seem to be agreed by all are that Winnie-the-Pooh is a glutton, and that Owl is full of pride.

The attempt to analyse character in terms of one particular predominant sin is clearly an exercise pregnant with difficulty, even with children's literature. And there is no reason to suppose that this simple one-to-one matching should work. As Mary Midgley put it in her seminal book *Wickedness*, 'Like fever, spite, resentment, envy, avarice, cruelty, meanness, hatred and the rest are themselves complex states, and they produce complex activities.' This is a helpful observation and encourages us to move beyond the idea that these 'states' – whether we construe them as thoughts or sins, demons or vices – are the simple building blocks of our delinquency. They are more complex, inter-related and mutually entangled than that.

The point about thinking in terms of sins and vices is to help develop an understanding and interpretation of the dark side of the soul. Any analysis of what goes on in there is bound to be provisional, just as any attempt to catalogue the most important sins and vices is going to be subject to the relativities and contingencies of the day the exercise is done, the year in which the day falls and the pressures exerted by current affairs and recent history. Also, any analysis of the detail is going to be in some ways inadequate, and any list of sins and vices incomplete, in all probability revealing, through the obvious omissions the blind spots, if not the besetting sins, of the compiler.

The problem with the admirable and wise tradition that goes back to the early desert hermits of trying to understand ourselves, warts and all, through these complex and diverse yet simply named states, thoughts or passions is that the promising, creative, humane and therapeutic start that was made became, despite the lively variety that persisted through the medieval period, ossified in a definitive list that was needed for purposes of discipline and control, and where all questions of diagnosis and therapy were removed from the self to the external and authoritative agency of a hierarchal priesthood. Such systems as this need objectivity so much that they will construe and construct it even when it is not there. This is why the generative and positive legacy of problematic passions and hostile pleasures evolved over the centuries into a forensic list of seven deadly sins that were assumed to provide an adequate analysis of the dark side of the soul for all time.

It is curious, or pleasingly ironic, depending on your personality and perspective, to note that this corruption of the problematic passions approach is just the sort of thing that characteristically happens with some of the problematic passions themselves. The basic idea or drive is good, and the fundamental aspiration is blameless or even praiseworthy, but when it is taken too far it is corrupted and corrupting. The dark side of the soul is shadowy but not pitch black. It is dusk, not midnight. It is alive, not dead. It is dynamic not static. Unless we approach it expecting it to be lively not only in its own activity but also in protecting the murky darkness that characterizes it, we will be misleading ourselves in ways that are dangerous, irresponsible and unwise. It really is not so simple in that dark place.

Exploring the dark side of the soul by examining a contemporary collection of sins and vices does not imply that there are no other ways to study the causes of human behaviour, attitude and thought that are damaging and destructive – the pathologies of relational persons. On the contrary, this project is about thinking through the way in which these complex states work, looking at their internal logic and their relational dynamics, and pondering in particular their capacity to undermine, diminish or even destroy the very person of whom they are a part. It is intended to complement and allow for a more sophisticated dialogue with moralistic, legal and medical approaches to the subject by drawing on introspection, theological reflection and lay observation. We will not, by the end of our exploration, have caused the dark side of the soul to be fully floodlit. But some of the shadows may have faded a little, and we will have given some of the demons a fright by pointing a torch in their direction.

3

Naughty, But Nice

Several commentators have observed that the operative meaning of
'sin' in our time has become trivial self-indulgence. Among them,
Francis Spufford has put it most directly and trenchantly in his book
Unapologetic:

> Everybody knows, then, that 'sin' basically means 'indulgence' or
> 'enjoyable naughtiness'. If you *were* worried, you'd use a different
> word or phrase. You'd talk about 'eating disorders' or 'addictions';
> you'd go to another vocabulary cloud altogether. The result is
> that when you come across someone trying to use 'sin' in its old
> sense, you may know perfectly well in theory that they must mean
> something which isn't principally chocolatey, and yet the modern
> mood music of the word is so inconsistent that it's hard to hear
> anything except an invocation of a trivially naughty pleasure.

Like several other writers who seek (as I am doing) to revitalize our
understanding of sin, Spufford has in mind the advertising slogan
'naughty but nice' created by Salman Rushdie when he was an
advertising copywriter, and famously used by Lyons to advertise Mr
Kipling's cakes. The point of the advertising slogan is not only that

the attractions of 'nice' outweigh the threat of 'naughty', but that the question of whether or not to buy and eat a cake is one that simply boils down to whether you want to. The alliterative phrase really is very clever. 'Naughty' is an archaic word. If it is used at all these days it is to describe childhood misdemeanours and the humiliating punishment that follows – a spell on the 'naughty step'. And 'nice' is a word that seems pleasant enough but is often a cloak for all sorts of nonsense and nastiness that in the end undermine the aspirations of those who seek to be – nice.

The question, then, of whether there is more to self-indulgence than harmless pleasure is a good one with which to begin to explore the dark side of the soul. After all, if it is simply a den of nice naughtiness we may as well simply enjoy ourselves. On the other hand, if there are some pleasures that are potentially problematic or even hostile, then we have every reason to handle our pleasures with care, and to remain vigilant even when having fun.

Gluttony

In some ways, gluttony is a perfect example of the complex and insidious nature of sin.

Clearly we have to eat to live – so, what's the problem? It's not that we have an appetite for food. Indeed, eating and drinking are good things, vital for health, part of the joy of social gatherings and integral to rites of passage. Within the Christian frame of reference, eating is important in the ministry of Jesus and ultimately defines the relationship between Jesus and his disciples: 'Take, *eat*; this is my body.' Christianity is, in fact, remarkably positive about food and liberal about what is eaten. Consider this passage from Mark's Gospel:

> [Jesus] said to them, 'Then do you also fail to understand? Do you not see that whatever goes into a person from outside cannot defile, since it enters, not the heart but the stomach, and goes out into the sewer?' (Thus he declared all foods clean.) And he said, 'It is what comes out of a person that defiles. For it is from within, from the human heart, that evil intentions come: fornication, theft, murder, adultery, avarice, wickedness, deceit, licentiousness, envy, slander, pride, folly. All these evil things come from within, and they defile a person.'

It is hard to imagine a religious pleader taking a more liberal attitude towards food. Not only are all 'clean' but neither gluttony nor greed are seen anywhere on the list of 'evil intentions'. To this day, Christianity has far fewer food restrictions than other religions and encourages a grateful response to the provision of food in ways that range from Harvest Thanksgiving to grace at meals. The Lord's Prayer includes the request for daily bread – one of the least troubling of petitions in any prayer in any religion, for who does not hope that there will be bread every day? And at the heart of Christian spirituality is nothing more esoteric than a meal, albeit one transformed by thanksgiving, remembrance and fellowship – the service of Holy Communion, a foretaste of the heavenly banquet.

Fasting is also part of the Christian tradition, but it is by no means as important as it is in Islam or Judaism. It is not seen as an obligation or duty, and while it is understood in a highly attenuated way, giving up chocolate or some other mouth-watering delicacy for Lent is more properly adopted as part of a positive package of spiritual disciplines. The other two aspects are prayer and almsgiving. All three of which are loosely derived from Jesus' time in the wilderness and the temptations that ensued. None of this denies the goodness of food or appetite, but it does raise the question of whether or not there are any limits on the goodness of grub and eating it.

The medieval theologians were not inclined to be especially hard on those who were prey to gluttony. Dante locates gluttons near the top of purgatory, just one level below the promiscuous. He has them treated with ironic retribution, doomed to a pig-like squalor while seeing (and presumably smelling) in the tantalizingly close near distance the very delights that they used to enjoy, and now relentlessly crave. But he clearly doesn't feel that this is a terribly bad sin. For Aquinas it is certainly one of the deadlies, but his concern, as it so often is, is with the problem that when our appetites and emotions drive us, our rationality – in his view, our more God-like faculty – loses its proper dominance. This reliance on a model of human beings – a psychology, if you will – that understands people to be good to the extent to which the rational will imposes itself, is a main weakness with Aquinas' approach as far as modern people are concerned. There are two problems. First, it is simply too cognitive. Second, it is too interested in control.

For now it is significant to note that for Aquinas the problem of gluttony is not one of quantity, but quality. Like Evagrius, he is concerned not with those who shovel down the calories but with those who are picky and choosy, preferring the choicest cuts and most delicate of morsels and seeking them out. Simon Laham makes fun of this, calling Aquinas' gluttony 'the sin of the French', and suggesting that without it we would be bereft of most gastronomic pleasures, a truth that doesn't entirely eliminate the possibility that there *is* sin in gluttony. And the sin of gluttony is not only of a self-indulgent kind but also one of depriving others of the benefit of enjoying their fair share of the earth's bounty, or perhaps even of their own harvests, sending food that has become fashionable to distant markets rather than growing the basics to feed their children; not to mention what the French anserine community would say to humanity about their experience of enforced gluttony in the service of our gastronomic delectation in the form of *foie gras*.

It might nonetheless be fairer to see Aquinas' gluttony as a monastic kind of sin. Monastic life involves subjecting oneself to the rigours of community life, in the Christian West usually in some kind of settled institutional life following the Rule of St Benedict or something similar, or a more rustic and nomadic life after the model of St Francis. Both forms of monasticism will be deliberately tough on those for whom the pleasures of the personal palate are particular priorities. In the one case because the whole conventual enterprise relies on the economies of scale made possible by common life. There is no *à la carte* at the refectory in a real monastery, nor much scope for notifying the kitchen of dietary preferences. In the other case the problem is not so much of scale, as of the commitment to poverty. Begging for food was the early Franciscan paradigm, as it is in Buddhist and some other monastic traditions. No form of monastic life makes it impossible for monks or nuns to be gluttonous, however. Medieval monasteries grew famously rich and the communities could enjoy security and a lifestyle beyond the imagination of the peasants in surrounding villages. Plenty of opportunities for gluttony arose, as they always do when people prosper. Similarly, the pragmatics of begging sooner or later inevitably begin to take over from the ideals of sustained vulnerability, and at least some friars would find themselves seeking scraps from rather well-appointed tables that in the fullness of time they would develop the knack of sniffing out. Friar Tuck is an all-too-believable legend, especially when one considers the uncertainty of life on the missionary road.

This, perhaps, has little of a direct nature to say about the experience and reality of gluttony today, but it is a helpful exercise in imagining what one might call the *entropic* quality of sin and vice more generally. It really is very difficult to stamp out sin or eradicate vice, even if we create cultures and lifestyles and communities that seem, on the face of it, to have the express intention of doing so.

Turning our attention to the question of gluttony today raises a host of difficult issues, of which gastronomic fussiness seems to be the least of our worries. The most obvious issue is the obesity epidemic that is such a major factor in the Western world, not least among children. As I write this, it is announced that over the last decade there has been a 60 per cent increase in the number of people diagnosed with type-2 diabetes. Significant numbers of people, perhaps the majority of the population, do not have a healthy balance between the number of calories consumed and the number expended. Not every individual case is as simple as that; there are some hormonal conditions and so on that cause people to become obese on quite modest diets, but clearly there is a major 'relationship with food' thing going on in our culture. Moreover, there is a connection between obesity and poverty in the developed world. This is very surprising to those who come from a subsistence economy, and remains counter-intuitive to many. It certainly doesn't mean that poor people are having the best food or the most meals. What it means is that disadvantage is complex and that trying to move from cause to effect in short steps or in straight lines is not often likely to do justice to a situation involving human beings and their appetites and desires. It may even be that one person's gluttony, in the sense described, leads to someone else's obesity, through the complex machinations of the market and the pressures created by the advertising industry. The importance of issues such as access to good education about food, and the availability of a balanced range of foodstuffs at affordable prices, cannot be overstated.

We also live in an era when eating disorders are prevalent and known to have complex causality. Among them are factors such as distorted body image and a desire to exercise control over at least one aspect of one's life when feeling pushed around or bullied. At a less medicalized level of cultural life, it is well known that the propensity of people to undertake special diets, whether on one's own initiative or because advised or counselled to do so, is extensive, and the organization Weight Watchers, which provides some basic information about nutritional needs with the monitoring of personal weight, has been hugely successful.

There are two ways of interpreting all this. The first is to realize that to start to use words like 'gluttony' in this environment is to throw a lighted match into a firework factory. There are subtle and serious sensitivities here. A ground-breaking book on eating disorders was called *Fat is a Feminist Issue*. Maybe there is a need for a book entitled *Food is a Spiritual Issue*, the point being that we need to develop (or perhaps regain) a rich and deep understanding of the way in which we let our appetite for food, which is expressed both in personal cravings and through economic systems, lead us personally and collectively into situations that are problematic in many ways. There are matters of justice here as well as of health, responsibility as well as freedom. This is not just about food and me, it is about God and us. Gluttony is an area that is obviously far more complex than either following one's natural appetites or eating what is put in front of you.

A final point is more chilling. It is that an obesity epidemic, coupled with a rise in eating disorders and, dare I mention it, unprecedented interest in television programmes about food, is exactly what you might expect to find in a culture that has lost contact with the wisdom that is somehow enshrined in the notion that gluttony is a deadly sin.

Intoxication

What do you make of these words of a Cambridge University anthropologist who has turned his gaze not on some remote and exotic tribe, but on the life of his own college?

> There is a saying that, 'A scientist is a device for turning coffee into theorems'. And there is indeed a high emphasis in Cambridge on liquid stimulants – coffee, tea, beer, sherry, wine and port. The role these play in the sociability and creativity of an institution like Cambridge are worth considering.

The careful analysis that follows examines the different parts that coffee, tea, beer and wine play in the life of the university. The social side of drinking these different liquids is a study in its own right, but the intoxicating elements of them all, according to our anthropological guide, are also important parts of what makes Cambridge intellectually productive. Coffee spurs the tired student or researcher on into the night; tea is 'consoling, relaxing, invigorating and restoring'. Not only has the process of boiling water for tea killed unnumbered gazillions of bacteria that would otherwise have laid many scholars low over the years, but it has been shown to improve 'the memory and associational powers of the brain by up to 20 per cent'. When it comes to beer, it is in 'the huddled charm of a busy bar' that 'difficulties, blocks, puzzles seem to resolve themselves' and 'the imagination is released to play more intuitively with hypotheses'. And then wine – '*in vino veritas*' – 'in wine, truth'. Our guide believes this one, and explains that what happens at formal dinners is that a sense emerges that 'one can speak the truth, be honest, close the gap between the constantly watchful self-control of ordinary life, and one's real feelings. One can tell the truth more directly, and learn truths that would normally be kept hidden.' Summarizing the effects of beer and wine the anthropologist couples together their relaxing and intoxicating effects, seeing them as 'an alternative to walking, having a shower, gardening, sport and all those other devices for altering our viewpoint on the world'.

Such is the positive side of drink. But there is a darker side too; alcohol, at least for some, is an addictive drug and its impact on health, conversation and behaviour is by no means always positive.

'Please drink responsibly' says the label on the bottle. But people don't always do so. Some will always drink irresponsibly, seeking in *vino* not *veritas* (truth) but escape, or even oblivion.

Then there are the drugs that people smoke. Tobacco and cannabis spring to mind and have many features in common, with cannabis being apparently less addictive and having very positive analgesic properties for people with conditions such as multiple sclerosis. A big difference between the two in many countries is that one is legal and the other illegal. One raises considerable sums in tax revenue, the other has a market of almost £4 billion annually in the United Kingdom alone. This is highly charged territory; there are those who have lost their jobs for saying that cannabis is less harmful than some legally available drugs, and others who believe that the case against cannabis – that it really is addictive and can precipitate depression or psychotic conditions such as schizophrenia – is mounting.

The question of the *legalization* of drugs is one that is often discussed. But perhaps the proper question is the *prohibition* of drugs, because everything is legal until prohibited. In Britain there has now been about a hundred years of prohibition, but it began to be pursued vigorously only in the 1960s. Indeed, amphetamines that were banned in 1964 were issued to soldiers in the Second World War, about 70 million tablets altogether being dispensed. Since the Misuse of Drugs Act of 1971 there has been a huge rise in the use of illegal drugs. Today more than half the population in their twenties and thirties have taken illegal drugs. Town centres often have small outlets of 'legal highs', many of them 'new psychoactive substances' which are similar enough to familiar drugs to have the same effects, but sufficiently different to slip outside legislation. This is a lucrative business that has caught the eye of those concerned for the welfare of the vulnerable and the good order of society. Whatever else prohibition does, it doesn't make the problem disappear. In fact, the effect seems more like giving an overgrown bush a good pruning; it reinvigorates growth.

The question of what to do about drugs is one of many contemporary social and political questions that former Home Secretary Charles Clarke believes to be intractable for contemporary politics and governance processes. In an essay in his book *The Too Difficult Box*, Alan Howarth examines the issues that need to be navigated if the harm that may be inflicted by drugs is to be reduced. The way in which he sets the question is informative, and intentionally avoids the framework set up by the strategic slogan 'war on drugs'. In this he is following the lead of countries like the Czech Republic, which found that clamping down hard on drug users increased drug use, and Portugal, which found an approach based on de-penalizing the possession and use of small amounts, investing in education and treatment and developing 'Dissuasion Commissions' to be very effective.

If the war on drugs cannot be won by prohibition and prosecution it seems entirely correct to think of another way of dealing with the negative side of intoxication. Such a way will inevitably devolve more to the softer processes of interpersonal influence and self-control. Education will be integral to this, and while an atmosphere that is not dominated by prohibition will make a far more conducive pedagogical environment, it will not, as if by a magic wand, make individuals any more able to cope with the negative aspects of intoxicating drugs, whether these be long-term health effects, a slide into addiction and all the personal, relational and economic consequences that flow in its train, or indulging in some of the behaviours to which intoxication can lead, whether they be foolish, harmful to others or personally dangerous.

The question of intoxication is a complex one, clouded not only by the phenomena themselves – different intoxicants impact differently, and different people respond differently to different intoxicants – but also by customs based in history and culture and by the consequences, intended and unintended, of introducing and prosecuting prohibitive legislation. But is it possible to cut through all this to identify some questions about the dark side of the soul?

Let me suggest the following.

First, is intoxication itself a toxic form of self-indulgence? This would be the sort of question to emerge from the deadly sins tradition. A few decades ago people would speak of their use of tobacco or their favourite alcoholic drink as their 'vice'. It sounds archaic now, and few in mainstream Christianity would argue for 'teetotalism' as a requirement on membership, or a *sine qua non* of discipleship, though there are a range of reasons why some people will avoid strong drink as a matter of principle. And yet the 'demon drink' does seem to have the form and structure of a typical sin or vice: that of a pleasure that can do good but can also go wrong and do far more harm than good to the person concerned and their wider circles of relationships; a hostile or potentially problematic pleasure *par excellence*.

A second set of issues that connect intoxication with the dark side of the soul concerns where responsibility lies for ameliorating the negative aspects of intoxication while allowing the pleasures, and promoting the positive side. In 1987 the Methodist Church of Great

Britain discussed these matters and agreed that all Methodists had a number of interconnected responsibilities regarding alcohol. Their list is worth quoting in full as it provides an interesting example of the way in which a serious group of people try to manage the various claims and dangers involved in dealing with the problem of a hostile or potentially problematic pleasure.

All Methodists should:

- consider seriously the claims of total abstinence;

- make a personal commitment either to total abstinence or to responsible drinking;

- give support wherever possible and by appropriate means to those who suffer directly or indirectly from alcohol misuse;

- unite to support pressure on government and public opinion for a programme designed to control consumption and reduce harm;

- recognize the importance of example and education in family life;

- where they practise total abstinence take special care to avoid authoritarian attitudes which may be counter-productive;

- where they practise responsible drinking take special care to demonstrate that this also involves self-controls.

The same report agreed that the Methodist Church should actively engage 'in the promotion of responsible attitudes to alcohol and in the support (whether directly or indirectly) of those suffering the harmful consequences of their own alcohol misuse, or that of others'.

This is a long way from a *laissez-faire* or merely hedonistic approach to alcohol. This particular list does not identify the 'claims of total abstinence', and while it may seem an odd phrase to some, it is the approach that many take when it comes to other drugs. It is also noticeable that the second bullet point is based on an ethics of personal commitment. Again, this is not something to be taken lightly, but to be thought through carefully. There are distant echoes of Aquinas' approach to sin and vice here. Aquinas believed that the deadly sins were inadequately controlled desires and passions, and that it was the role and duty of reason to bring such self-indulgence or 'concupiscence' to heel. And there are echoes of Paul's dualism that presents the body and its appetites as the problem.

We are a long way from the life of a Cambridge anthropologist fuelling his late-night writing with caffeine, and oiling the intellectual and social life of the college with beer and wine; and in many ways that is a pity. There is a tendency in those who take sin seriously not to take it quite seriously enough, or to think it through in the round, both realistically and deeply. This is the natural consequence of taking the 'transgression' model of sin as the norm: there are good things that you should do and bad things that you should not do, and it's your job, or the job of the authority figure to whom you sequester your conscience, to know where the line is drawn, and then to police it vigilantly. Life is then just a matter of avoiding the vices and practising the virtues, rather in the way that young children will sometimes try to walk only on the paving stones and avoid the cemented joints or cracks between them. Or, to put it in terms of another game, of hoping to land at the bottom of a ladder rather than on the mouth of a snake.

Such pictures, models and metaphors seriously underestimate the sophistication of sin and vice and the subtlety required of mature human judgement. In particular, they fail to recognize that a vice is not typically something that we need to exclude, prohibit or exorcize, but something with which we need to develop a critical and constructive relationship. That is, we must learn to live with our vices; in particular, we need to learn how to flourish while acknowledging that we cannot eradicate them from ourselves or others. Such an observation suggests that it is better to avoid prohibition as far as possible, and to encourage all members of society to take personal responsibility for their decisions, not as isolated individuals but as relational people, depending on others to help them to be wise and, when they are not, to cope with the consequences. To do this involves more than proffering state-provided education and social support; it requires communities committed to the common good and a common mind that doesn't divide the population into good people and bad people but that sees everyone as potentially good, probably harmed, certainly in need of friends and genuinely capable of making a positive contribution to the whole. Life can be rendered negative not only by self-indulgence that has harmful consequences, but also by the unnecessary denial of positive pleasures, and a cultural inclination to seek to eradicate things that will never go away. The 'war on drugs' will never be won until we recognize that it can't be won and we choose a different approach. That approach is to reconcile ourselves to the dark side of the soul while not capitulating to it.

To do this involves asking how we might manage our vices, our potentially problematic passions, by a combination of self-awareness and developing a realistic, constructive and inclusive cultural ethos that affords support to those who are more vulnerable to the hostile or toxic aspects of some pleasures. To generate the resources to do this on a cultural scale would involve disinvesting some of the resources currently committed to managing sin and vice by regulation and punishment.

Talkativeness

Talking to excess may seem like an unlikely sin of self-indulgence. After all, some people talk very little and some talk a great deal. Neither is especially good or bad. Perhaps we should just relax about how much people happen to say.

Such a view is not one that will be easily adopted by a person who has been subjected to the relentless onslaughts of someone for whom thought leads to speech in a way that fills so fully the available time that no one else gets a word in edgeways and the speaker never becomes a listener. Wise parents might say to their children that they have two ears and one mouth, and that they should use them in that ratio. For the same reason the Orthodox iconographic tradition depicts saints with small mouths and large ears. But all this is surely at the level of chitchat. It is hard to imagine any real harm in yapping.

It is certainly unusual to find references to garrulousness in the great hamartiological works of the last millennium or so, although Gregory of Sinai, who lived in the thirteenth and fourteenth centuries, had it on his list in his work *On Commandments and Doctrines*, using the Greek word *polulogia*, meaning 'much speaking' or 'loquacity'.

More significantly for the English-speaking world, among the fifteen most celebrated sermons preached by the eighteenth-century philosopher, theologian and bishop, Joseph Butler, one is entitled *Upon the Government of the Tongue*. This, while a little antique to our modern ears, says more than enough on this subject to convince me at least that talking too much can be just as corrosive as eating or drinking too much. So let's see what he said at the Rolls Chapel back in the 1700s.

The sermon is based on the short sentence in the letter of James which says in the Authorised Version of the Bible that 'If any man among you seem to be religious, and bridleth not his tongue, but deceiveth his own heart, this man's religion is vain.'

Butler begins by asking what this means. Is James talking about the need not to lie or deceive in speech? He argues that this is not the point at all. The tongue, like any other part of the body or human faculty, can be used for all sorts of good or evil purposes, but that is not what is at issue. 'The thing here supposed and referred to', he asserts, 'is talkativeness', which he defines as 'a disposition to be talking, abstracted from the consideration of what is to be said; with very little or no regard to, or thought of doing, either good or harm'.

It is inevitable that those inclined to the folly of talkativeness speak about many trivial things. This should not, however, lead us to the conclusion that the fault is a trivial one. The trouble is that once trivial matters are exhausted, which eventually they are,

they will go on to defamation, scandal, divulging of secrets, their own secrets as well as those of others, anything rather than be silent. They are plainly hurried on in the heat of their talk to say quite different things from what they first intended, and which they afterwards wish unsaid; or improper things, which they had no other end in saying, but only to afford employment to their tongue.

Butler emphasizes that the problem with talkativeness is not that we go out of our way to cause trouble to defame others, but that *the habit of talkativeness leads us in the direction of doing so unwittingly*. He contests that 'this unrestrained volubility and wantonness of speech is the occasion of numberless evils and vexations in life'. And he goes on to paint the following picture:

> The tongue used in such a licentious manner is like a sword in the hand of a madman; it is employed at random, it can scarce possibly do any good, and for the most part does a world of mischief; and implies not only great folly and a trifling spirit, but great viciousness of mind, great indifference to truth and falsity, and to the reputation, welfare, and good of others.

While harsh about talkativeness, Butler is very much in favour of *conversation*. He was a serious man and so he sees the need to communicate thoughts in order to carry on the affairs of the world. He believes that the first purpose of speech is to increase knowledge and learning, and allows that it also serves to delight and create enjoyment too. Conversation is, he says, 'social and friendly, and tends to promote humanity, good nature, and civility'.

But the gratification of conversation, he argues, subsists in its *mutuality*. He quotes the wise teacher of Ecclesiastes saying that 'there is a time to speak and a time to keep silence', but adds that, 'one meets with people in the world, who seem never to have made the last of these observations'. And of such he suggests that their conversation is merely the exercise of their tongues: 'no other human faculty has any share in it'. For Butler, conversation is relaxation, the opportunity 'to unbend the mind'; it is 'a diversion from the cares, the business, the sorrows of life'. And yet, 'Attention to the continued discourse of one alone grows more painful often, than the cares and business we come to be diverted from.'

It is interesting to see how Butler's reflections connect with the advice of various pundits and gurus today. Those who advise on communicating effectively would echo his point that people render themselves, and what they have to say, insignificant by excessive talkativeness: 'insomuch that, if they do chance to say anything which deserves to be attended to and regarded, it is lost in the variety and abundance which they utter of another sort' is his way of putting it. Those responsible for the remarkable TED talks have simply changed the rules of giving a lecture, insisting on no more than eighteen minutes. It's the same point.

In the final part of his sermon Butler reflects on the dangers in what he calls 'discourse of the affairs of others, and the giving of characters'. He is talking about gossip.

It is a subject racked with difficulty and Butler shows himself to be a lay psychologist in his observation that 'There is perpetually, and often it is not attended to, a rivalship among people of one kind or another, in respect to wit, beauty, learning, fortune; and that one thing will insensibly influence them to the disadvantage of others, even where there is no formal malice or ill design.' This might seem to suggest that we should avoid the subject of other people at all costs, as we are likely to be speaking on the basis of motives of which we are not properly aware. But Butler does not advocate complete silence on the qualities of others. It is too important that 'the characters of bad men should be known'. In other words, if someone is a reprobate or a deceiver, or if someone has evil intentions on others, it is not your duty to remain silent on the subject – that is *not* good governance of your tongue, it is a failure of duty. Nor is it a duty to be taken lightly; Butler is aware of the consequences of speaking ill of those who are in fact good. Yet it remains important. And although Butler does not make this point, the existence of this duty reinforces his earlier point. If you need to denounce a character you can do so much more effectively if your habit is *not* to speak ill of others. Here endeth a lesson from the eighteenth century on what is now called 'whistle blowing'.

Butler goes on to make the happier point that it is a much less serious error to speak well of someone undeservingly. It does no immediate or particular harm; though it should not be something we do to excess for reasons already abundantly clear.

These insights of Butler, expressed in the language of the eighteenth century, are perhaps as relevant today as they were in his day. Back then the world was relatively silent because the only way people communicated was by speech or written word. In our digital age the opportunities to produce and communicate words are endless. We have access to mobile telephones, tablets and laptop computers with unimaginable computing power, and an apparently limitless number of television and radio channels. Social media channels give us all the opportunity to become broadcasters, sharing our observations, judgements, boasts, grumbles, witticisms and cautions with potentially endless numbers of people. It is the nature of social media that people enter into them in a light-hearted way. That is part of their charm, just as it is part of the charm and delight of friendly conversation. But Butler's warnings about the way in which it can all too easily go wrong if we allow ourselves to be unreflective as well as unremitting transmitters is apposite. Light-heartedness can quickly become irresponsibility if we are in the habit of seeking to get a reaction rather than to convey a truth.

As I write this, new examples come to light on a regular basis. The case of Sally Bercow, whose seven-word tweet about Lord McAlpine was judged to be highly defamatory at a High Court hearing leading to a payment of 'undisclosed damages', is probably the most famous to date. After the judgment, Bercow's QC issued a statement which said 'Mrs Bercow wishes and hopes that as a result of this matter other Twitter users will behave more responsibly in how they use that platform. She certainly intends to do so herself.' The point is not to bridle the tongue but to restrain your tweeting finger. The two are undoubtedly connected – both to each other, and to the dark side of the soul.

We live in a time when being outgoing, extraverted and bubbly is praised and prized. The case for 'Quiet' is harder to make, though it has been well made in a recent book of that name. The case for silence and reserve is also difficult to make convincingly, though the need for both seems ever more apparent and manifest, if we are to be able to listen, to observe and to attend to the truth and needs of others. There is a deep wisdom, not in sullenness, sulking or hostile silence, but in recognizing that at the moment I do not have anything particular to say or that, as yet, I do not have a contribution to make to this subject. Waiting in patient silence may be integral to the process of coming to say something not only worth saying, but also worth hearing. As has already been suggested, if we don't talk all the time people may actually listen to what we most want and need to say. It is a good technique when speaking in public to leave a little pause of silence before an important point. Oddly it's the silence that regains people's attention.

It is not always important to have something to say. On the contrary, it is far more important to know when you do not have anything to say, and then the wisdom and courage to say – nothing. Talking too much is just as much a vice as other forms of self-indulgence. We enjoy it at the time, but it ends up doing more harm than good, both to others and to ourselves, and perhaps most sadly of all, we very rarely notice that we are doing it.

4

Vicious Regards

In this chapter we look at five attitudes and habits, two of which have held positions of prominence, if not eminence, for as long as people have been thinking in terms of deadly sins and vices: vanity and pride. No one seriously believes that it would ever be possible to eradicate these from our character, but then again no one seriously believes that all pride is bad or that vanity and vainglory can never serve positive purposes. Nonetheless, there is sin and vice here, and we will do what we can to uncover it. The fourth part of the chapter is about abjectness, which is not something that Christian leaders, to their shame, have often gone out of their way to discourage in others. Abjectness is a genuine vice, despite the fact that it is often presented as humility – a very significant and important virtue. But seeming to be like something is not the same as being something – if it were then the word 'fake' would have no meaning. And finally we come to envy. We begin, however, with snobbery.

Snobbery

'There is no doubt', writes Judith Shklar in a footnote, 'that the use of the word [snob] in its present sense became very frequent from about

1850? The word is much more ancient than that, and in the Middle Ages it apparently meant 'snivelling'. But why 1850? As it happens, 1850 is just two years after William Makepeace Thackeray published his *Book of Snobs*, a wonderful satire on those who look down on their social inferiors. In it he satirizes the observations, habits and judgements of every kind of snob he can imagine; military, royal, university, clerical, Irish. The chapters appeared first in *Punch* and the style is light and engaging. And they were timely. The emergence of snobbery in this sense was part of a wider cultural and social change in the mid-Victorian era. The old established hierarchies were creaking, but still persisting, as were values that kept a somewhat feudal mentality in place while the tide of liberal democracy continued to rise.

Snobbery would probably not be able to exist in a society that is entirely egalitarian, or one that is completely hierarchical or utterly totalitarian. It comes into being when people are confused and insecure about how to rank each other, and yet not sufficiently relaxed to avoid trying to do so. It is a ready source of comedy because of the absurdity and irony of snobbery. Snobs place a high value on appearance, and yet assume that their own vanity is invisible. They draw attention to themselves without realising that their self-regard is their most evident characteristic.

So let's enjoy some Thackeray.

The word Snob has taken a place in our honest English vocabulary. We can't define it, perhaps. We can't say what it is, any more than we can define wit, or humour, or humbug; but we KNOW what it is. Some weeks since, happening to have the felicity to sit next to a young lady at a hospitable table, where poor old Jawkins was holding forth in a very absurd pompous manner, I wrote upon the spotless damask 'S – B,' and called my neighbour's attention to the little remark.

That young lady smiled. She knew it at once. Her mind straightway filled up the two letters concealed by apostrophic reserve, and I read in her assenting eyes that she knew Jawkins was a Snob. You seldom get them to make use of the word as yet, it is true; but it is inconceivable how pretty an expression their little smiling mouths assume when they speak it out. If any young lady doubts, just let her go up to her own room, look at herself steadily in the glass, and say 'Snob.' If she tries this simple experiment, my life for it, she will smile, and own that the word becomes her mouth amazingly. A pretty little round word, all composed of soft letters, with a hiss at the beginning, just to make it piquant, as it were.

Jawkins, meanwhile, went on blundering, and bragging and boring, quite unconsciously. And so he will, no doubt, go on roaring and braying, to the end of time or at least so long as people will hear him. You cannot alter the nature of men and Snobs by any force of satire; as, by laying ever so many stripes on a donkey's back, you can't turn him into a zebra.

There are many types of snobbery and Thackeray's story here illustrates the pompous sort, which is not perhaps the most pernicious, and might be connected with vanity rather than anything worse, though on the evidence of this story alone we cannot decisively say that Jawkins was not arrogant or narcissistic. He certainly didn't seem to be paying much attention to his conscripted audience.

Snobbery involves making judgements on the basis of the wrong information. We can laugh when we see others do it, but perhaps fail to notice when we do it ourselves. Thackeray makes much in his first two chapters of the social response that might be made to people eating peas with a knife or picking their teeth with a fork. The reader may ask whether, even in these days when cutlery is seen as an option when certain foods are on the table, or bought to take away from a shop, they would have a hint of a response to such behaviour if they witnessed it at a café or restaurant. And whether, if there was a flicker of response, it might lead to a sense of superiority in oneself.

Since the middle of the twentieth century, the language of snobbery has been overtaken by that of prejudice, and it has moved on from being a matter of taste, decency and amusement to an affront against justice and social inclusion. Rather than Thackeray's comedy of Victorian snobberies, we now have to wrestle with the serious matter of equal opportunities. In our common mind today to fail to respect and promote that worthy ideal is far more serious a matter than 'sin', just as to be exposed as a racist is not to be seen to be in possession of a vice, but to be – well it's hard to say what – a disgrace, a pariah, or a demon to be cast out. I make this point not in order to praise racism, but to hint, as delicately as I can, that even the most heinous of unreasonable, prejudicial attitudes, those which make life a misery for others and prevent the proper development of a flourishing society, are quite possibly to be found somewhere on the dark side of the soul of even those who protest against the evil itself. Racist, me? Well, perhaps.

We may make our society less racist, and pray God we will continue to do so, but this does not mean that we are personally free of racism. Judith Shklar lists snobbery among her 'ordinary vices', a term she uses to refer to 'the sort of conduct we should all expect' rather than exceptional causes of harm and evil. She also insists that the ordinary vices have both personal and public dimensions. This is precisely what we see in racism – and in all the other -isms of prejudice. It is the ordinariness of these vices that proves that we cannot tidily divide the world into 'racists' and 'non-racists'. It may be a bit annoying, humiliating and embarrassing to admit it, but racism, snobbery and the like are probably similar to other vices and sins. We don't think that there are some people in the world who have lust and some who do not; nor do we think this of gluttony, or rage, or pride. So might we think similarly when it comes to racism? If we do not, then perhaps we will begin to think in a more puritanical way, and raise the spectre of modern Puritanism, which, like old Puritanism, is very likely to be based more on repression and self-deception than on candid self-awareness.

The dark side of the soul doesn't go away just because we disapprove strongly of what is lurking there. Indeed it is our disapproval, our sensitizing, our moral education that is potentially one of the reasons why the lights do grow dim in that part of ourselves we used to think was normal, proper and good. When one British comedian met the local vicar after his mother's death to prepare for the funeral, he was asked if she had any hobbies. He replied that she was a very committed racist. For the atheistic comedian this had the desired effect of creating an excruciatingly awkward moment for the hapless cleric. It is one that illustrates my point precisely. The terrible thing about the prejudices that are now so demonized is that there was possibly a time when we, or our parents or grandparents, were relaxed and comfortable in holding them.

Me, a racist? Me, a snob? Well, perhaps I used to be, when more under the influence of Mum and Dad, or maybe the grandparents, back in the day before we realized this was wrong. When we think of the attitudes that were once acceptable and are now deplorable we are tempted to what Wendell Berry calls 'historical self-righteousness', which we could think of as a form of moral snobbery. We like to suppose that had we lived in the bad old days we would have behaved better than our forebears. And yet, as he rightly puts it, 'The probability is overwhelming that if we had belonged to the generations we deplore, we too would have behaved deplorably.' This is not the worst of it. Looking forward with moral imagination we have to accept the wise but chilling truth in Berry's next sentence. 'The probability is overwhelming that we *belong* to a generation that will be found by its successors to have behaved deplorably.'

We are unlikely ever to be as free of prejudice as we feel we should be, and would like to be. Aspiration and idealism are not good guides to the dark side of the soul. Unless we are very careful, our desire to be good can make us less candid even to ourselves about our weaknesses and flaws and vices. Well-developed and pernicious racism has been a terrible stain on recent human history, implicated in the slave trade and Holocaust as well as apartheid and the like. But to say that there are social and political situations where racism is manifest and must be removed from the civil ordering of society is not the same thing as saying that every racist impulse can or ever will be removed from even the most liberal and well-meaning of hearts, or that we will ever be able to view the ethical universe from the highest moral ground. We long for it, of course, but it is when we think we have reached it that we are at our most dangerously deluded.

The reason for naming snobbery as a sin is to hint at the truth of this, even though it is perhaps among the least acceptable propositions in this book. Which is itself very odd. Why might it be that people are able to admit to gluttony, lust, arrogance and avarice but not to accept that in truth they really do feel a little bit superior to certain groups or categories of people or, if not that, to certain individuals. Why might it be that the typical behaviour of the snob, which is catchily and accurately summarized in the phrase 'kiss up, kick down', is not recognized as the sort of behaviour that is not exceptional but strikingly common, even if a little difficult to observe because we don't often see the same person in both kissing and kicking mode; unless, that is, we spend quite a lot of time with them, or unless that person is actually our self.

Snobbery, in both its comic and its unacceptable forms, is precisely the sort of thing that needs to be on a contemporary list of vices. Evagrius may not have named the demon 'snob'; he may never have felt it appropriate to look down on one hermit or up to another just because he knew something shameful about their past or because he liked some rumour he had heard about them. These are absurd notions because part of the point of the hermit movement was to move away from other people, and to avoid company and all the spiritual distractions it brought. The hermitage managed sins of other-regard by making it difficult or rare to regard others at all. Religious *communities* were a different matter, because their complex social arrangements made social and relational demands on their members. In Benedict's Rule we see much to encourage egalitarian mutual regard. Normal social distinctions are subverted by his requirement that even the youngest should have a say when decisions are to be made, and by his insistence on the importance not of rank but seniority, based on date of entering the monastery, and of the greater significance of role or office than matters of status or class.

It is in the melting pot of modernity that the demon of snobbery found that its hour had come. You might even say that in a liberal society we are all, inevitably, snobs. It's part of the way we cope. We are not very much aware of it, because snobbery involves paying less regard to that which we consider less valuable. Like several other sins and vices it's actually quite hard to catch yourself at it. In some cases that is because our capacity to self-excuse is so well developed, but in others, and this is a prime case, it is because we don't, or perhaps can't, notice that we look with an eye of pity and contempt on one, while squaring up, smiling and maybe gently bowing to another, and in many cases doing what we like to think we do *all* the time, which is to look them in the eye as an equal, or give them the precise dignity and respect that they need to fulfil their role and function. Think about it. Would you know if you were a snob? The same question applies to being patronizing – a genteel hobby of snobs.

Thackeray's work is a wonderful ramble through the vanities and hypocrisies of the snob classes. It's not just for laughs, however, even though he himself could not have seen the connections that we have made here between the harmless comedy of manners and some of the most wicked happenings of the last century or so.

I will let him have the last word.

I believe such words as Fashionable, Exclusive, Aristocratic, and the like, to be wicked, unchristian epithets, that ought to be banished from honest vocabularies. A Court system that sends men of genius to the second table, I hold to be a Snobbish system. A society that sets up to be polite, and ignores Arts and Letters, I hold to be a Snobbish society. You, who despise your neighbour, are a Snob; you, who forget your own friends, meanly to follow after those of a higher degree, are a Snob; you, who are ashamed of your poverty, and blush for your calling, are a Snob; as are you who boast of your pedigree, or are proud of your wealth.

Vanity

Consider for a moment something that William Makepeace Thackeray could never have imagined: the phenomenon of the television talent contest. The format is always much the same. Vast numbers of people are screened and then asked to perform their party piece in front of a studio audience, an expert panel, and the rest of us at home, who watch from the cringing safety of our sofas, from whence we challenge the opinions both of the expert judges and our fellow viewers in the room.

It is a huge spectacle, and a popular and lucrative one. These events are the very definition of 'prime-time TV' and are all the evidence we need that vanity, and its aspirational partner fame, are alive and well in our time.

When was it that 'fame' became such an important value? A recent broadcast of a children's choir at the BBC Proms featured an interview with a young member of the choir who, when asked to describe the experience, did not talk about the delight of musical performance but said, 'it was like being famous'. The point here is not to criticize her level of articulacy; journalists' questions about how something feels in the heat of the moment are among the most unfair questions going (and if this book were longer there might be a chapter about them). The point rather is that 'being famous' seemed to provide the girl with the most immediate and compelling frame of reference for a worthwhile and enjoyable experience. If this is true it is an at least noteworthy, if not eyebrow-raising, development of social values, and an extraordinary change that has happened in the course of just a couple of generations. One could hardly imagine the girl's grandmother saying something similar had she sung under the baton of Sir Malcolm Sargent. It is as if the quality of a performance is judged by its capacity to lead a person to fame; the by-product being seen now as the end that gives value to the means.

Andy Warhol once prophesied that the day would come when we would all have our fifteen minutes of fame, and perhaps we shall. As a parish priest preparing for a funeral, I have sat with enough bereaved relatives desperately trying to offer an account of the worthwhileness of the life of their loved one (itself not the point of my visit at all, but that's what some of the recently bereaved want to do: prove that a life was not lived in vain) to know that they often dredge up the moment when granny had her picture in the local paper or was in the company of a VIP. At the very first funeral I conducted, the music chosen was 'Roses are Blooming in Picardy', which even to this day I can't hear without recalling that the deceased on that occasion was in her youth once 'Rose Queen of Stretford'. The recollection brings a sentimental tear to my eye, and reminds me that not all sins require of us censorious disapproval. And vanity is just such a one.

We would be lost without vanity. Romance would be over, and there would be no amateur dramatics to amuse us on a lonely Saturday evening in the autumn. Vanity, like all the vices, is necessary not only to drive the fashion industry but also to make us house-proud enough to maintain reasonable levels of domestic order and hygiene. I was mildly amused when a friend told me that his teenage son or daughter (I don't recall which) had learnt a lot about personal grooming by joining the Sea Cadets, but in retrospect I feel that my amusement was misplaced. Seeing that someone has taken care about their appearance gives at least a suggestion that they care about the social environment they are entering, and that they respect the others who will be there, and the common purpose in which they are engaged. Or so I like to think. Perhaps King Duncan in Shakespeare's *Macbeth* is saying more truth than he knows when he says 'There's no art to find the mind's construction in the face.' There is more to the truth of a person than the impact of vanity on their appearance, though it is hard not to give credit to people for making an effort to impress.

Living and working in an academic community is an interesting context in which to discover how respect and vanity take different forms, and if I am sometimes unsure about how much mutual respect is in the room, I am never in doubt about the presence of vanity. Gabriele Taylor suggests that vanity can often be a mistaken and ultimately hopeless attempt to address a sense of personal inadequacy.

they are insecure in their self-evaluation, and to compensate look for a shallow substitute which cannot provide what they need, and cannot allay their anxiety. Their overriding desire, to gain esteem though presenting the 'right' appearance, makes them akin to the envious in that the means they adopt towards fulfilling this desire cannot provide what they are looking for.

Vanity is tragic because it simply cannot deliver deep satisfaction. But that doesn't stop it being a pragmatic means to worthy ends. Vanity and presentation can be a vehicle for self-respect and other-respect. In this way vanity differs profoundly from boasting, which is closer in spirit to the vice of vainglory – which was on Evagrius' list of eight 'dangerous thoughts' or 'hostile passions', though it was collapsed into pride by subsequent writers.

When we boast we talk up or even broadcast our achievements, our triumphs, our successes and our paltry victories over our insignificant personal weaknesses. All this seems to me to be a more apt and common expression of vainglory than taking care over one's appearance, despite the truth that to care too much about one's looks is not to care wisely. There can be visual as well as verbal boasting, and, unlike beauty, boasting is precisely *not* in the eye of the beholder, but in the intentionality of the would-be beheld. Should the reader at this point be thinking of a 'selfie' that is transmitted to the world via social media, or the re-tweet of a word of praise or admiration, or a Facebook post advertising one's recent success, then I would have to admit that they are following my drift quite accurately.

Curiously, the word 'vainglory' has more or less disappeared from the English language precisely at the time when there is more vainglory on display than ever before in history. I say 'curiously' but this is precisely what we should expect when we have developed a few insights into the dark side of the soul. Our passions and demons thrive and flourish best when they are not noticed; and so it is when a word drops out of the vocabulary that we give the demons the most fertile darkness in which to do their wicked work. I mean this seriously, even though I am putting it pictorially or metaphorically. We hardly have the vocabulary, never mind the counter-cultural courage, to critique the ravages of vainglory today. It may not be the worst cultural loss imaginable for the word 'vainglory' to have slipped from normal usage (imagine if we lost the words 'cruelty' and 'abuse', or 'injustice' or 'meanness'), but it is certainly not a positive situation to find ourselves in.

Vainglory is not a sin about doing the wrong thing, but about doing things for the wrong reasons – whether or not they are good or bad in their own right. Should vainglory, say the desire for flattery or approval, lead us to do something that is wrong, then we are doubly at fault, but should we do something that is worthwhile simply in order to be seen then it is vainglory that has undermined our virtue. This is quite a serious problem for members of missionary religions, who seek by their actions to witness to their faith and thereby to the God in whom they believe. On the whole, however, the New Testament is not encouraging about vainglory. For instance, when Jesus was tempted in the wilderness, one of the temptations was that he should throw himself from the pinnacle of the Temple and rely on God to save him. Jesus resists this, not for Health and Safety reasons but because it is wrong to test God in this way. He might just as well have said, 'because it is wrong to make a spectacle of your own faith'. When he taught about giving alms he said, 'do not let your left hand know what your right hand is doing', and his instruction on prayer was to do it in private. Vainglory is the opposite of modesty, and Jesus is teaching modesty here; the importance of doing things that are worthwhile in their own right, not because of the impression they make on those who see them. As soon as you get into that you make other people into your audience (which is to put them to use, not to relate to them) and then you start letting their expectations, their hopes, their need for entertainment – and this is the worst bit, their need to be impressed by you, shape your behaviour.

It is in such ways that vainglory slowly but surely captivates the person who is not able to resist its charms. The consequence: life lived on the surface, a frantic competition for a place in the local hall of fame, a desperately ugly struggle all round for the oxygen of publicity, and a vague but very real, sad and sinking feeling that we live in days where integrity and authenticity are in short supply, and fame and celebrity are near the top of the tree of values, and that we are all inflicted with a seemingly fatal dose of status anxiety.

Fame at any price is the tragic apotheosis of vainglory. It may seem to be a form of putting yourself above the crowd, but the reality is that it makes you vulnerable to the whims of the crowd. And as we have seen, one of the subtle and nasty things about vainglory is that it makes a negative out of a positive, and turns virtue into vice. Consider these scenarios:

You are modestly attractive. People comment. You work to improve your appearance. You get more attention. Soon you are dependent on your own looks for something core to your identity.

You are reasonably intelligent and hard-working. You achieve some modest success – get to a good university or a prestigious college. You have to work harder there but you still manage to float to the top. You are lauded and awarded and before you know it you are manipulated by your own success into thinking that above all else you must maintain this admittedly glittering image. To do so consumes your energies and you are never able to settle into a loving relationship but are seduced by the fawners, the flatterers and the other admirers who seek not true love but reflected glory. But reflected glory – or rather reflected vainglory – is a very unsatisfying basis for a relationship. So it doesn't last. Rather the demonic cycle of loneliness is perpetuated.

And so it is that vainglory coaxes us away from sustaining core virtues like service, truth-seeking and humility. Indeed, it introduces us to the lowest, most pathetic and destructive of idolatries – worship of the self or self-idolatry. The desire for fame, for repute, to be held in high regard, to be admired for our physical, intellectual or spiritual qualities, to be noted for our acts of service and kindness, all this seems natural only because the demon of vainglory is so subtle and pervasive in its influence today. It has hidden itself by making itself omnipresent.

As Gabriele Taylor clarifies, there is something sad, or even tragic, about the efforts made by those consumed by vanity.

The dominant feature of a wholly vain person is her absorbing concern with her appearance. Interest in how she appears is interest in the effect she has on others ... Where there is such a gap [between appearance and reality] the vain will tend to spend much time and energy on appearance which is designed to hide from others and also from herself the less acceptable reality.

Today we tend to feel that vanity is not a major vice, and vainglory is perhaps only a very minor failing, so to succumb to it is an acceptable weakness rather than anything that matters. But maybe this is to treat vanity too lightly. Although it is not the direct or immediate cause of anything spectacularly bad, it is a spider that spins a very complex and tangled web of tiny filaments. Perhaps it would be better to think of vanity as a starter sin, of vainglory as an entry-level vice. The slippery slope starts with the one-eyed, self-admiring glance in the mirror, and the anxious follow-up thought that others may not be so easily impressed, and the mistaken feeling that this really matters.

Pride

A major problem with the traditional list of the seven deadly sins is the place that it gives to pride. I refer here not to the criticism of the notion, which has come so trenchantly from feminism, that pride is the primary and most deadly of sins, though that is indeed a significant issue to wrestle with as we try to think through the difference between virtue and vice for people in different locations in the same culture. The problem is that pride has several, if not many, faces. In a previous book I distinguished between good pride and bad pride, and here I am focusing only on bad pride, which comes in various forms such as arrogance, conceit, hubris and chauvinism. Vanity is perhaps the most superficial form of pride, so shallow that it is in fact not pride at all but a *desire for good pride* that seeks to develop it in misguided and ultimately self-defeating ways, as we have seen.

'Arrogance' is the closest English word we have to the Greek word 'hubris', which is often translated as 'overweening pride'. The arrogant are not interested in flattery or fame because they do not believe that the admiration of others, on whom they look down, is of any significant worth. One of the features of the hubristic in Ancient Greece was that they would desecrate the bodies of those defeated in battle. This is deeply distasteful to us, and provokes a visceral revulsion; in a word, disgust. And yet to the hubristic it is entirely compatible with the contempt in which others are held. There is aloofness here, and the defeated enemies are trashed for the worthless refuse that they are believed to be. This is very different from respecting one's valiant foes in their defeat, but also very different to advertising one's formidable prowess to others. It is essentially, and this makes it even more revolting to us, play.

The conceited are in many ways like the arrogant, and it is therefore reasonable and helpful to think of them both as 'proud'. Both believe themselves to be superior to others, but, unlike the arrogant, the conceited, like the haughty, *do* have a regard for others, for it is by comparison with others that they know themselves to be better. The conceited are not at all indifferent to success and failure. On the contrary, it is by learning to succeed that they have got where they are today. The problem for the conceited is primarily that they have inhaled the heady oxygen of success too deeply and have come to the view that their own abilities are in a comprehensive way superior to those of others. It is for the potentially conceited that Rudyard Kipling wrote the poem 'If'.

It is therefore conceit that is the most important form of pride for us to consider, as while few of us are arrogant in the thoroughgoing sense that I have described above, many of us have developed at least a little conceit. Moreover, the truly arrogant would be very unlikely to pick up this book. Their problem is not that their soul has a dark side but that it has a sizeable pitch-black area of which they are completely unaware. The arrogant therefore know little of self-awareness or its ugly twin, anxiety. In some ways their lot is enviable, but what makes it so is not the truthfulness of their perception and perspective, but their imperviousness to evidence. There is no true contentment for the arrogant, but there is extreme complacency. Their apparently enviable happiness is, alas for them, short-lived.

The one thing that most threatens the arrogantly proud is the thought, or idea, of God. While in a colloquial way we might say that the arrogant envy God's ultimate superiority, the truth can also be expressed more theologically. God, and only God, makes the truly arrogant anxious. The only strategy then for the absolutely pride-filled, such as Milton's Satan in *Paradise Lost*, is to go in for a radical reversal. The solution to this awful and unwelcome conundrum is to fall, or perhaps to dive down, rather than to float near, but not at, the very top, and to revalue radically. This is precisely what Milton's Satan does when he cries out, 'evil be thou my good'. And herein is the terrible sting. For evil, being nothing, cannot be good. The descent and fall of Satan is the descent into nothingness. He moves from proximity to the light to the deepest darkness. He takes what he can with him, but there is no possibility of community, enlightenment or advance where he is gone. This is hell – not an alternative value system, but *no* value system. Not dastardly knowledge, but dull ignorance. Not edgy company, but no company. Not dodgy mates, but no mates. *Pace* Jean-Paul Sartre, hell is precisely not 'other people'. Hell is deep loneliness. In fact the most accurate thing to say would be that hell is what happens when relationship becomes impossible, when the self contradicts its own fundamental relatedness.

It is thinking along these lines that is all of a piece with the notion that arrogant pride is the most grave of the sins. But you don't need the mythology (or indeed God) to make the argument. Gabriele Taylor argues this out psychologically, starting with the apparently impregnable self-knowledge of the arrogant who have 'no need for reassurance'. However, 'far from indicating a sense of security such moves rather point to a refusal to face at all the issue of an esteem-worthy self. Maybe this entitles the arrogantly proud to hold the position of exhibiting the deadliest of all vices.'

This is heady and extreme stuff, and a long way off, one hopes, from the everyday life of the reader of this book. Conceit, however, and narcissism, and the desire for status – such things are much closer to home and are far murkier, which in this context is actually a good thing as murk (or, in its medieval form, 'mirk') is a more enlightened state than the deep darkness of satanic pride.

One area of life in which the snares of conceit and narcissism are particularly evident is that of *leadership*. The reasons for this are straightforward. It's not that the conceited tend to find themselves in leadership positions. It's that when people find themselves in leadership positions they are mostly likely to think that their position reflects their significantly superior capacities. That's half the story. The other half is that sooner or later narcissistic and conceited leaders realize to their horror that there are competitors and critics out there who are just waiting for them to slip or expose their weaknesses. This provokes anxiety, and when leaders are anxious they become self-conscious and defensive with regard to their weaknesses. A spiral begins whereby they seek neither the advice and suggestions, nor the analysis and solutions, of their colleagues. Rather they begin to shut down their perceptual apparatus and rely on their own inner genius, forgetting, just when they need to be most aware of the fact, that they have their limits and that their own soul has a dark side.

This sort of scenario is typically called 'hubris' today. The meaning is mercifully less extreme than the ancient Greek form, and is usually a version of conceit rather than of arrogance. And this conceit is not all internally driven. The problem for the hubristic (in this sense) is not excessive self-belief but that they lack a sufficiently robust infrastructure of character (one could call this 'down-to-earth-ness' or 'humility') which might, if it were present, have ensured that their status and responsibility did not destabilize them. Manfred Kets de Vries writes that the hubristic have a dysfunctional form of self-love, and that they see only what they want to see, which is aggravated by the fawning of their closest followers. This fawning and flattery then becomes a need for them, a 'heightened desire for admiration'. As a result they systematically cut themselves off from the kind of colleagues who would give them helpful advice, criticism and feedback. This all has the kind of shape and dynamic of development that we have seen before. It is one of the classic shapes of a vice or sin. And it gets worse. The hubristic ignore the needs of others; they are really turning in on themselves now, in order to achieve their own ends. As Kets de Vries put it, 'Vindictive, contemptuous and impatient with others, they react with disdain, rage and/or violence when a situation is not to their liking.'

The viciousness of this process is palpable when described like this. It is in the nature of vice to hide itself, and so as hubris grows, self-awareness diminishes. For this reason it is more than likely that many who read the passage above will immediately think of others; their boss perhaps, or their boss's boss. However, on the off-chance that this seems to be the sort of thing that might just be intensifying the darkness in part of your own soul, it may be worth asking whether there could be any way of breaking this spiral once it has started. The answer to that question probably depends on how long you have been spiralling hubristically into anxious and pompous isolation. If it's not too late, you can always do the most sensible thing when faced with the feeling that vice is tightening its grip, and that is to talk to someone who will listen to you with kindness, courtesy and respect and then say, again with kindness, but also with candour, what you need to hear. On the other hand you may feel this to be the most ridiculous suggestion that you have ever heard; after all, no one else would understand. In which case the advice is much simpler. Resign!

Which brings us on to the important question of why it is that feminism has been so critical of the idea that pride is the deadliest of the deadly sins. Surely the argument laid out above is persuasive: the problem is that pride ultimately cuts us off from community, alienates us from ourselves, and plunges us into the complete darkness of ignorance. And all this without the theological superstructure that says that pride is wrong because it is a failure to recognize that God is God.

The problem that feminism has with pride, however, is not in terms of the understanding of what it can do, its deadliness in that sense, but in its prevalence in any particular community, and in the extent to which prohibitions on pride, when put forward by the powerful, can inhibit the flourishing of the oppressed. Pride is never without a context, and for most if not all of Christian history that context has been patriarchy, a system of oppressive thought and practice into which pride has been inextricably woven, not as a way of sowing a seed of doubt in the oppressive but as a way of keeping people in their hierarchically determined place. It is easy, straightforward and correct to accept this point. There is a real problem if, in a hierarchical context imbued with inherited prejudice, uneven distributions of power, and precious little mutuality, the word from the top is 'first, watch your pride'. Indeed, this is the sort of abuse of position for which satire was invented. Having seen how hubris is the besetting sin of the anxious leader, it is easy to apply a little hermeneutical suspicion and suggest that maybe all this anti-pride talk from powerful narcissists needs to be turned on its head. Pride is not the besetting sin of the many, but the fatal flaw of the few at the top.

The problem, from a feminist perspective, is the proposition that the root of all sin is discontent with one's lowly social position and limited options. The feminist argument is that what women need to hear is not a message about the dangers of getting above yourself, but a message about the dangers of not fully being or realizing yourself. This is a good argument and is true not only for women, but for all oppressed people. And that is why a discussion of abjectness immediately follows this brief reflection on bad pride.

Abjectness

The word 'abjectness' is unusual. It's not often you hear of someone complaining about someone else's abjectness or wondering whether they themselves are 'too abject'. If we hear the word at all these days

it is because someone has offered 'an abject apology'. This is the sort
of apology that people offer when they realize that they are in the
wrong and have run out of excuses, so that, without a leg to stand
on, they grovel. This is grovelling with good reason. The sin, or vice
of abjectness, however, is grovelling *without* good reason. In terms of
the vocabulary we are using here you could call it vicious grovelling.

Discussing the sin of abjectness, or calling it a vice, doesn't feel
very comfortable, because we think that the abject have already done
themselves down more than enough and we shouldn't put the boot in
when they are on the floor, or collude with their own poor estimation
of their worth. Such discomfort is well meant, but it is neither wise
nor appropriate. Calling abjectness a sin is not intended to load more
problems on to the abject; it is simply to call a spade a spade. It is
never tactful, especially in our own day, to refer to anything as a sin
or a vice. But tact isn't the issue here. The whole point of this exercise
is to try to come clean about where the dividing line between what is
good and what is sinful can be drawn; to clarify what is a virtue and
what is a vice; to distinguish between a positive nurturing quality that
will build us up, allow us to flourish, and serve the common good in
the long term, and the habits and attitudes that diminish us and may
ultimately destroy us.

And abjectness certainly does not fall on the positive side of
that line.

Another problem with talking about abjectness, perhaps, is that it
is a vice that looks rather like a virtue. And not just any old virtue, but
humility itself – what Hildegard of Bingen called the 'queen of virtues',
a view shared by a very different woman thinker, the philosopher and
novelist Iris Murdoch.

Abjectness is the opposite of arrogance, but that doesn't make it good either. Aristotle famously developed and popularized the idea that a virtue is the mid-point between two vices. This isn't always the case, but it is in this area. Just as bad pride, be it conceit or arrogance, is a vice of self-regard, so too is abjectness. It is wrong to think less of yourself, to underestimate yourself, to think that you are somehow inherently less worthy or worthwhile than others. Humility is no more the virtue of doing yourself down than it is the virtue of puffing yourself up. It is the virtue of being yourself naturally and comfortably, and of relating to people in such a way that you encourage in them the same straightforward, honest decency. It is the Goldilocks spot where someone is neither too abject nor too arrogant.

One of the problems with being abject is that it is a state of mind that is very concerned about status and difference. Like conceit it is contaminated by vainglory or, 'status anxiety'. These matters are not really worthy of our preoccupation; they deliver little by way of reward and distract us from far more important matters. Certainly we have to take them into account and navigate the various positions and roles that others and we may have. But these are matters that we should try to deal with in a deft and skilled way, not in a self-conscious and energy-sapping way. Status anxiety is not to be confused with role clarity, for instance, even though different roles are valued differently. What matters is not that someone performing a lowly function knows their place or shows deference, but that they perform their role well, and that there is mutual respect between all who have a role to play in the enterprise. In an organisation where roles and responsibilities are carefully assigned should someone in a lower position assume the responsibilities of someone in a higher position then there will be trouble, but so too will there be trouble if someone in a higher position assumes the responsibilities of someone in a lower position. Integral to a cooperative community is a combination of role clarity and mutual respect. Abjectness, conceit, vainglory and status anxiety are all vicious, and among the things they undermine are the true foundations of collaboration and community.

To change our focus from the functioning organization to the vagaries of social life raises the question of what used to be called good manners, and common courtesy. André Comte-Sponville considers politeness to be the first of the great virtues on his famous list. It is not the most exalted virtue (that is love) but the most basic and fundamental; one without which we are much hampered in any attempt to live relationally, never mind virtuously. The point is not to make a fetish of who we are and where we fit into any of the multiple structures that we inhabit, but to develop the skills that mean that we don't constantly have to be thinking about it. This is just as true if we want to change things as it is if we are happy with the way things are. The problem with abject people, like conceited people, is that they constantly drag the background material that exists to make organizational or social life functional – a proper sense of modesty, humility and respect for others and so on – into the foreground and thereby corrupt it. Many of the apparently abject are actually faking their abjectness, performing it for manipulative reasons, or simply because they are mistaken about the nature of politeness or respect, seeing it through the lens of vainglory rather than that of community and service.

Abjectness is a vice partly because it is so unwise, and partly because it is actually a bit obsessive. We have yet to consider the sin of control, but abjectness can be something of a control issue. Abject people insist that this stuff about status really does matter, and the fact that they apparently do this at their own expense convinces us for a while, but in the end only aggravates the suspicion that they are up to something.

We considered at the end of the previous section the feminist critique of making pride the primary sin. Looking at this argument again, this time through the lens of abjectness, or false, forced or *faux* humility, might make us wonder where we would be as a culture if, rather than preaching against pride, the Church had fought the good fight against grovelling abjectness. The truth of the matter is that there are two connected, but equally vicious states of mind here, both for the subject, and for all they come across. In fact, given the choice between having to deal with an extremely conceited person and a deeply abject person I am not sure which I would prefer. It is easier, however, to have a laugh about the conceited, perhaps because, as Jesus said of those he accused of hypocrisy, we know that they have already had their reward. Yet just to make that comment makes me wonder – what might the reward for abjectness be if it isn't part of some wrong-headed strategy of interpersonal manipulation?

This is where we begin to reveal the truly sinful nature of abjectness. There are several levels to this. At the first level abjectness is to do yourself down and pretend that you don't have anything much to offer. This is an affront to your own dignity and to the common good. To the abject of the world I say, 'stand up and make your contribution. It's no good leaving all the talking to the talkative and conceited. We need you!' At the next level of abjectness there is, I want to suggest, though with some trepidation, sometimes a bit of inverse conceit, a bit of 'actually, I think I *do* have a singular contribution to make but I can't be bothered to make it', or, 'really and truly I couldn't care less' in the attitude of the abject. To say this is to make a connection between abjectness and the acedia family of sins that we will consider in chapter 6: apathy, sloth, boredom and the like.

A habit of abjectness is not the only reason why some people never flourish or make the contribution to the common good that they might. There are many reasons why some are voiceless, and the oppressive use of power, whether deliberately and consciously or habitually, or through inherited social structures, is often important. But again there is a challenge. Acquiescing is not good enough, either for you or for your children, who will suffer the same fate as you unless someone stands up to be counted. Abjectness is not only the vice of deference where it is not due, but the collusion with unjust practices of exclusion. Abjectness is among the vices because it cannot lead to personal or communal flourishing. We could no more have a happy flourishing community of the abject than we could have a happy and flourishing community of the arrogant.

Some may protest that this whole section hasn't begun to address the most important question, which is the matter of self-esteem. That's true – in a way. We are not using that language here, as it is technical and caught up with a different discourse. It is axiomatic that when people are abject it is often because they have been treated badly in the past or because they have been socialized into it. But sin- and vice-talk is fundamentally the language of personal responsibility and accountability, not causality or explanation – or even self-improvement. The reason we talk about vices and sins is to goad people into taking the counter-cultural risk of assuming more and not less responsibility for who they are and what they are like. This is a fundamental aspect of what it means to talk about being a sinner. It is the only way to make sense of the curious notion of original sin. This is not the time to explore all the strange metaphysical byways opened up by that doctrine, but the pragmatic imperative remains: talking about sin, vice and virtue invites people to take responsibility for their own attitudes and behaviours, both with regard to themselves and in regard to others.

Reflecting on abjectness and identifying its dangers is a vital part of coming to terms with the 'pride' family of sins – the 'vicious regards'. It helps clarify the nature of true or virtuous humility and to reframe the critique of 'pride'. It also reveals that the influence of vainglory is deeply insidious not because the abject act in vain or vainglorious ways, but because they see the world through vainglorious spectacles and are therefore victim to the same misperception as the vain and conceited. These vainglorious lenses distort value perception so that status becomes overvalued and mutual respect undervalued. As a result, the abject inappropriately seek a place of low status rather than attempt to live lives of genuine and fulfilling service while paying little regard to irrelevancies and accidents of status. There is indeed irony in this, and it is this unrecognized or unthought-through irony that is part and parcel of the manipulative agenda of the abject.

The message to the abject is this: find the confidence and encouragement to grow into the person only you can be. At the end of your life no one is going to praise you for your grovelling and abjectness, nor does anyone love you for it now. Nor do you like it in yourself. It's time to get over being down on yourself. There is a long way 'up' for you to go before you risk getting proud, pompous and conceited, so let yourself drift a bit in that direction. You will be surprised how good it feels, and how much your true friends respect and love you for doing it. For one thing, you are likely to be, and to have, a lot more fun.

Envy

The seven deadly sins are sometimes divided into two categories – the hot or bodily ones and those that are more cold-blooded. Envy is traditionally understood as a cold one; unlike lust, anger and gluttony but like pride, greed and sloth. This doesn't mean that we don't feel our envy deeply or suffer from it profoundly. But there is more than one type of envy and even obsessive envy is not beyond transformation.

Our first guide to the complexities of envy is Gurcharan Das. Das was a highly successful Indian businessman until he took what he called an 'academic holiday' when he was fifty. Seeking to enrich his life in a different way, he took himself off to Chicago to study the Hindu Scriptures in Sanskrit. Finding new fulfilment in studying, reading and writing, his academic vacation became a way of life, giving him an interesting vantage point from which to reflect on a number of matters, among them one that is deeply connected with the theme of this book and admirably summarized in the title of one of his:

The Difficulty of Being Good. In it he considers a number of virtues and vices by engaging with the Sanskrit epic the *Mahabharata*, and seeking to illuminate *The Subtle Art of Dharma* – the subtitle of the same book. When he begins to discuss envy, Das suggests that maybe it is not a bad thing but a good thing, not a vice but a virtue. This is the view his father took, seeing it as fostering a healthy competitive spirit. This view is not uncommon. It sees envy as the spur of positive aspiration and bold ambition.

Reflecting on this after years of a very successful business career, Das suggests that there are two types of envy. There is indeed a benign kind, the envy that spurs us on to do as well as or better than others. But he also found a form of envy that was pernicious. In particular he noticed that people envied and bad-mouthed those who were wealthy enough to be able to lend them money. He went on to write that, 'The envy I encountered in the business world, however, was nothing to what I would see later in the academic world.' He quotes Henry Kissinger's cruel explanation that the extent of the envy is because 'so little is at stake' and goes on to say that 'there is a certain misery attached to the academic life, no doubt, in which envy plays a considerable part'.

Joseph Epstein also reflects on envy in the academic world in his very readable little book on envy, suggesting that at the top of most academic subjects is a very small group of people who don't get on well because none can bear the thought that the other might get ahead. He also notes the point that should an academic write a book that happens to sell well they will be dismissed as a popularizer. According to Das, such mean-spirited envy is a great leveller. But it levels down, not up. 'Instead of motivating one to

better performance . . . envy prefers to see the other person fall. The
envious person is prepared to see both sides lose.'

Positive envy, that is the modest spur to do better as one's sense of
rivalry and competition has been sparked by the success of another,
seems to be a necessarily fleeting emotion. You hear of something that
someone has achieved, or maybe they have just been lucky, and you
wish that the success had come your way rather than gone to them.
But after a while the feeling dissipates, your attention goes elsewhere
and you get over it. It was 'transitory envy', not an admirable emotion
but neither one that is altogether toxic. This is not the same as negative
envy, which has more than a tang of resentment and bitterness about
it, and which causes you to focus in a hostile way both on what it is
that you envy about the other person and then on your active dislike
of them for having something that you desire. This second is what we
might call *vicious envy*.

In vicious envy we not only observe others, but let them get under
our skin. One of its features is that it is disproportionate. Vicious envy
is not roused by the most objectively enviable of people, but by those
who are closer to us, and with whom we have a great deal in common.
When people say they do not envy the Queen, or Bill Gates, or when
clergy tell you they don't envy the Archbishop of Canterbury, they
are telling you very little. No one *envies* these people, because they
don't identify closely with them. The person we envy is much closer
to home than that. It is the person who you would be if things had
worked out just slightly differently; if she or he had not happened
upon that smidgen of good fortune that was passing by when you
were not in the room. People sometimes marvel as the sibling rivalry
and other forms of domestic dysfunction that they find in the Hebrew

Bible. Why marvel? Who else was Cain going to envy than Abel? Who else could Saul envy but David? The point is that envy occurs most acutely between people who are close.

Gurcharan Das tells a comparable story from contemporary India. It occurs between Anil Ambani and his bother Shakuni. Both were very rich. But despite the fact that Anil was the fifth-richest person in the word, he was consumed by envy for his elder brother. And so he set out to destroy him. One thing that matters about this for us is that the accumulated power and wealth of these men meant that so much was at stake as the envy began to run its course. According to Das, their joint enterprises accounted for 3 per cent of India's GDP, 10 per cent of government tax revenues and 14 per cent of India's exports. The consequences if all this went wrong were on a massive scale; remember, we are talking about 3 per cent of *India's* GDP here and India is a huge country. But huge collateral consequences are of no concern for a person in the grip of envy; sense of proportion is often the casualty of being caught up in sin or vice.

In the end, the problem between the brothers was solved by the mother, who found a way of dividing the family company and putting more distance between them, and with that greater distance they went on to prosper way beyond even their wildest dreams. Das sees this as a story which supports the view that while envy can be dangerous it can also be motivating, and connects this with the Hindu teaching that says that Dharma draws a fine line between the positive and negative sides of competition. There is wisdom in this. We do not deal well with sin and vice if we think that it is always and only bad or that it is eradicable. Envy may not be very nice, nor is it logical or reasonable, and yet it is very common and unlikely ever to be excised from the human heart.

Others have said that envy is the saddest of the sins as it doesn't desire anything for itself; it just desires that someone else doesn't have a benefit that I don't enjoy. This is the meanness, or the mean-spiritedness, of envy that we so despise when we come across it in others – and in ourselves. But it's not just that envy is a negative feeling that we experience when someone else is more successful or fortunate than we are. We are perversely satisfied when we hear that someone we envy has fallen on hard times. This is an especially miserable aspect of vicious envy.

There is another side to envy: not being envious but being envied. 'It is better to be envied than pitied', they say, meaning that no one pities the fortunate. But being envied in the settled, hostile, obsessive way that I have identified as vicious is neither pleasant, nor noble, nor desirable. It is better to be admired than envied. Much better. Moreover it is better to admire than to envy, and to the extent that we can turn our envy into admiration, and perhaps let our admiration allow us to learn positive lessons from the example of others, we may have done something to move this aspect of the way we look at, think about and develop feelings towards others from the dark side of our soul to the bright side.

It is futile and self-defeating to pretend either to others or to ourselves that we never feel a pang of envy. The question is whether we recognize it and try to do something constructive with it, or whether we ignore it, let it settle, take root and then begin to spread like ground ivy. We have already seen that one constructive option is to seek actively to turn our envy into admiration. We might even think that we can share in some of the delight that the person who is the object of our envy enjoys in the status or achievement that we envy so much. To do this is to engage in a spiritual and emotional sympathy that doesn't have a specific word in English (which is perhaps rather telling) but is rather like a positive form of compassion. If compassion is 'suffering with', the word we need is one that refers to delighting-with or sharing-in-enjoyment-with: 'com-delight' or 'com-joy', perhaps.

Can we ever fully eradicate envy from our souls? Can we pull out all that spreading ground ivy? It seems very unlikely. But practical questions aside, my argument here is that it would be undesirable to excise it. There are worse conditions than envy; extreme aloofness or arrogance, for instance. The arrogant know nothing of envy, and it is more the pity for them because modest, fleeting envy can be so positive. Nor do the arrogant often admire those who are different, and not to admire others is a terrible poverty for any human being, any being that is fundamentally a 'relational self'.

Envy will never be finally eradicated from our soul, but it may be neutralized, or tamed, or trained to a worthy purpose, when we seek the fulfilment and flourishing of all, and desire ourselves to be of genuine service to others and to the common good. That's a very tall order and it is unlikely that we will ever achieve it. But if we do it will not be because we have avoided envy, but because we have acknowledged it, seen it for what it is – pathetic, demeaning and vicious – and ultimately transcended it.

Envy is inevitable, and in moderate and episodic form it can be good. Obsessive, vicious envy, however, is a very sad and very nasty sin. Left to grow, it kills happiness, desiccates personality, destroys relationships and distorts opportunities for learning and development. There is, however, a positive potential in envy, so we should not be too negative about envy in ourselves or draconian when we see it in others. If our envy can become the raw material that is transformed into admiration for the achievement of others or 'com-delight' in their good fortune, it will have served us well, and we will be on the way to being of genuine service to others and to the common good.

5

Impossible Ideals

Integrity is an important quality in a person, but is it overrated? Consider the following words in praise of integrity.

The single most important quality you can ever develop that will enhance every part of your life, is the value of integrity. Integrity is the core quality of a successful and happy life. Having integrity means being totally honest and truthful in every part of your life. By making the commitment to become a totally honest person, you will be doing more to ensure your success and happiness in life than anything else you can ever do . . .

Integrity is the foundation of character. A person who has integrity also has an unblemished character in every area of his or her life. One of the most important activities you can engage in, is developing your character. And one of the best ways to develop your character is by consistently doing the same things that a thoroughly honest person would do in every area of his or her life.

To be totally honest with others, you first have to be totally honest with yourself. You have to be true to yourself. You have to be true to the very best that is in you. Only a person who is consistently living a life with the highest values and virtues is a person truly living a life of integrity. If you are always honest and true to yourself you cannot be false to anyone else.

These words are written by 'A former ad agency executive and marketing consultant, [whose] work in personal development focuses on helping his clients identify hidden marketable assets that create windfall opportunities and profits, as well as sound personal happiness and peace.'

It would seem from all this that the author had never heard of 'original sin', the idea that we are always out of kilter, with the corollary that we can never quite sort ourselves out – even if we really seriously want to, even if we want to sign up to the programme that is being marketed here. Nor is there much space in all this for the thought that each and every human being has a dark side to their soul. Living with integrity, it is suggested, is just a matter of always doing the right thing for the right reason – QED. Go for it!

Put like this, the contemporary goal of integrity feels something like the more ancient goal of chastity. It sounds easy and straightforward, until you bring human beings into the equation. Then it gets complicated, as Augustine acknowledged when he wrote, 'Lord, make me chaste, but not yet.' The modern person might say, 'Lord, give me integrity, but it will have to wait until I've dealt with all the less than straightforward issues that seem to dominate my personal, professional and political life.'

The importance of integrity is not undermined by recognizing that it is difficult, or very difficult, or perhaps impossible, to achieve the highest standards of probity and candour. As we acknowledge the reality of the dark side of the soul, and begin to explore it, it is prudent and timely to see how it connects with the ideal of personal integrity and with other high and noble aspirations.

There are four sections here, all of which consider some aspects of the contemporary dance around the ideal of integrity. We start by considering the opposite and enemy of integrity – hypocrisy. Recognizing that hypocrisy is not quite as easy to avoid as we might at first have thought, we move on to consider the question of 'defensiveness' and the way in which, with more or less self-awareness, we actively hide the truth from ourselves. The following two sections consider two dreams of personal aspiration that are of particular importance today. The desire for certainty, and the hope that we might, like the 'former ad agency executive', know how to achieve the heights of personal perfection that we imagine for ourselves in our more idealistic moments.

Hypocrisy

Given how fierce Jesus is about hypocrites it is rather odd that hypocrisy doesn't rank among the traditional deadly sins. Jesus' real and uncompromising ire was kindled by the Pharisaic 'blind guides' who focused their attention on the externals of religious adherence. Matthew's Gospel furnishes several example of Jesus using the H-word to denounce people. Some are occasions when he attacks people for the show that they make of their religion.

> Whenever you pray, do not be like the hypocrites; for they love to stand and pray in the synagogues and at the street corners, so that

they may be seen by others. Truly I tell you, they have received their reward.

Whenever you fast, do not look dismal, like the hypocrites, for they disfigure their faces so as to show others that they are fasting. Truly I tell you, they have received their reward.

Going on the evidence of the text alone, it is not clear why the word 'hypocrite' is used here. After all, the pray-ers and fast-ers simply seem to be letting others know what they really are up to. At first glance it seems as if Jesus has got this back to front. It is those who pretend not to pray or fast while actually doing so who are guilty of play-acting, whereas it is those who let their feelings show, and project their spiritual earnestness into the social environment, who are demonstrating a simple continuity between what is going on 'in here' and 'out there'. Is Jesus not actually advocating hypocrisy when he suggests that the fast-er should smile though the pain of gnawing hunger?

The word 'hypocrite' is derived from the Greek word for the mask or 'persona' that an actor would hold in front of their face in a play. In essence, it is the sin of pretending to be someone you are not. There is, however, more to hypocrisy than impersonation or pretence, or for that matter playing a role. Social and organizational life absolutely depends on people playing roles, taking parts, inhabiting 'offices', in which certain behaviours are not only expected but required, and where it is reasonable to speak of the *performance* of duties. We expect it of people not to hold such roles if the value system in which the role is embedded, or the qualities associated with the personal office, are dissonant with their personal values or behaviours. To discover, for instance, that an equerry at Buckingham Palace is a staunch republican who gives much of his leisure time to supporting the local branch of the Socialist Workers' Party is to encounter someone carrying so much irony and dissonance that it is reasonable to think that they are being hypocritical. On the other hand, to work in a Nissan factory while owning a car made by Ford may be seen as an act of disloyalty, but it is not necessarily hypocritical. That co-workers might feel betrayed is another matter, but one that conveniently helps illustrate the complexity of the web of sin: hypocrisy is connected to vanity which is connected to loyalty and to betrayal and so on.

What, then, of our praying and fasting Pharisees; are they really hypocrites? Yes, but in a less than entirely straightforward way. Fundamentally, their problem is their *vanity*, or more precisely their vainglory or 'status anxiety', their desire to be admired. They esteem the appearance of what they are doing, and the regard that they get from others for appearing to do it, more than they do the activity itself. And as the activity is piety, or, as we might say today, spirituality, the authenticity of that very activity is undermined and for *that* reason it is hypocritical. If you make a show of singing a song to amuse and impress others then no one can quibble. It's one of the reasons that some people sing songs and others listen. If, however, you make a show of praying or fasting, or some other aspect of your inner life, then you have got things seriously wrong. And it is reasonable, especially if you are Jesus and not, say, Immanuel Kant, and your idiom is hyperbole rather than forensic verbal precision, to denounce this as 'hypocrisy' as part of your programme of critiquing and revising religious practice. Prayer, spirituality, piety, religion –

for these things to be authentic they must be entered into for their intrinsic value. As soon as they are done as a means to an end the activity itself is undermined. This is especially so if the end that the 'actor' has in mind is self-aggrandizement. 'Dress to impress,' they say. But not in religious garb, we might add.

To fast for the sake of being seen to fast is not to fast for the right reason. To pray for the sake of being seen to pray is not to pray for the right reason. Indeed, it is possibly not to pray at all, the desire to be seen undermining the honesty and vulnerability that is integral to true prayer. Jesus is not primarily addressing a disconnect between the inner and outer world when he uses the word 'hypocrisy' here. What he is doing is using a couple of examples of the way in which vainglorious self-regard, or narcissistic concern about the way in which one appears to others, undermines authentic spirituality. The praying and fasting are not genuine activities that happen to be observable because (say) lips are moving or the complexion is a little wan and facial features drawn. If they were they would not be hypocritical. They are hypocritical because they are performed for social reasons. The hypocrisy subsists in hiding the real or primary motives. It is to guard against this that Jesus recommends adopting forms of piety that cannot impress others, because they are invisible to the objective observer.

Another passage unearths deeper layers of hypocrisy.

Then Pharisees and scribes came to Jesus from Jerusalem and said, 'Why do your disciples break the tradition of the elders? For they do not wash their hands before they eat.' He answered them, 'And why do you break the commandment of God for the sake of your tradition? For God said, "Honour your father and your mother," and, "Whoever speaks evil of father or mother must surely die." But you say that whoever tells father or mother, "Whatever support you might have had from me is given to God", then that person need not honour the father. So, for the sake of your tradition, you make void the word of God. You hypocrites! Isaiah prophesied rightly about you when he said:

"This people honours me with their lips,

but their hearts are far from me;

in vain do they worship me,

teaching human precepts as doctrines.'"

The problem here seems to be that those who take it upon themselves to criticize Jesus' disciples do so by picking up on a detail of behaviour that is not unlike their own behaviour – except that their own break with tradition is a more serious breach. They are hypocritical because they are criticizing others for faults they could more readily and seriously identify in themselves. The embedded quotation from Isaiah goes even further, and points us towards one of the core problems with our most familiar form of hypocrisy – the disjunction between heart and lips, between what we ought to say and what we actually say. As we have noted, this is *not* at the core of Jesus' problem with hypocrisy. What he doesn't like is double standards, judging others using criteria that you decline to use in judging yourself.

Our interest here, however, is not in perfecting our description of objective hypocrisy, the hypocrisy of others, of which there is without doubt a hidden abundance, but rather with understanding our own hypocrisy; the hypocrisy that is our vice, and therefore somewhat hidden from us.

Let's begin by noticing that it is possible to see vice and virtue in the same behaviour, depending on whether we or others are the subjects. For instance,

I am *flexible*.

You are *accommodating*.

He or she is a *hypocrite*.

Or,

I aspire to *humility*.

You are making an effort at *modesty*.

She is simply *insincere*.

Or,

I am carefully *negotiating a compromise*.

You are *skilfully reconciling enemies*.

He is *compromising his principles*.

What would Jesus make of this inclination to praise ourselves and those close to us, but to criticize others for similar behaviour? It is hard to imagine that he would be impressed. His reason for raising the issue of hypocrisy was not to ask whether there are hypocrites out there in our community or in public life more generally, but to force his listeners to examine their integrity and to discover, in the process, genuine inner complexity – the murky muddle of the dark side of their soul.

But if this all seems very difficult let us for a moment consider something simpler: the charlatan, for instance. Charlatans are hypocrites, swindling people on the basis of some deception that they themselves don't believe in. This is bad faith, too obviously reprehensible to be worth reflection were it not for a theme that has more than once spiked our consideration of the sins and vices: that of the strange lack of accuracy and acuity in self-knowledge. So, to put it simply, there are charlatans and charlatans. Some quacks will be cynically peddling snake oil knowing that there is no basis for the claims on the bottle – and behold, here is a genuine charlatan! Others will themselves believe all that it says on the tin. These are gullible pawns working for some Wizard-of-Oz-type character behind the scenes. Not a true charlatan, but an unwitting fraudster. And then there are the others, those who should know better but for some reason manage to find themselves marketing snake oil not because they are sincerely convinced of its powers, but because they have managed to cut themselves off from the inner voice that is saying, 'Come on, you know this is nonsense.' And then there are yet more others who, while they know their product is not really what it claims to be, believe that it is at least *something* and well, to see the smile on the face of the person who, at least for a minute, believes that they might have just bought a cure for their painful ailment, or received a convincing diagnosis for their inner distress . . . that moment of hope has to be worth something.

Hypocrisy is the sin of those who lack *complete* integrity. But complete integrity, while admittedly tautologous, and proffered in simple terms by our 'former ad agency executive' as relatively easily achievable, is not something that we often find in a human being. It's an important ideal, but it doesn't do justice to the actual complexity of real people. Even when we say that someone has 'complete integrity' we don't mean that what you see is entirely and wholly all that there is. What we mean is that the person we are regarding has exceptional probity and remarkable authenticity. It is a figure of speech, and if we don't recognize that, we end up expecting too much of others and giving ourselves an unfairly hard time.

It follows that there is likely to be quite a lot of hypocrisy about. Does this matter? Is hypocrisy a vice, or is it just one of those things – a social necessity, a matter of pragmatic realism? After all, if we were to tell the people we live and work with the content of every emotion and passing thought that we have we would fairly quickly find ourselves becoming socially isolated. Domestic and cultural life depend to a considerable extent on the prudence of the bitten tongue as well as tactfully understated criticism and generously overstated praise. It is unlikely indeed that every primary school teacher really has a 'brilliant' class, with 'fantastic' pupils who do 'wonderful' work. And yet to fail to make such claims, at least from time to time, is clearly to fail to understand what is expected, indeed required, of a teacher today. We do not call those who over-praise for effect 'hypocrites' because it is hypocrisy in a noble cause. A teacher who warmly expresses that she is 'really proud of you all today Form 3' might actually be slightly irritated with one or two of them. She is, however, putting that irritation to one side so as not to spoil the opportunity for some positive reinforcement of better-than-average behaviour, and no one is offended or feels that she lacks integrity for being generous and generic in her praise. However, should the same teacher pretend to colleagues that her new class has responded to her really well, when in fact they have not, or that she is enjoying the challenge of a middle leadership when she is in truth reporting symptoms of stress to her GP, then an altogether different picture emerges.

We are, I suggest, living through a period of semantic inflation that requires of us that we avoid middle-order words and replace them with the extremes. This is one of the reasons why 'evil' has become a more common word, and why the subtleties of 'satisfactory', which I remember were the only nuance on my own school reports apart from the ubiquitous 'C – could do better', have been eliminated. The school reports of the mediocre old days were not besmirched by hypocrisy so much as rendered dull by teacherly sloth. It is 'really fantastic' that much more effort is being put in to provide feedback that can motivate, but when motivational language is a substitute for someone communicating an important truth then we have moved, it would seem, into the land of the hypocrites, where being economical with the truth is not only the norm but the most esteemed virtue. Indeed, there is an increasing body of evidence that excessive praise can inhibit learning and build up self-esteem to a deleterious extent.

The problem with hypocrisy is that it creates a false view of the world; it presents distorted truth. This is not only annoying for those taken in by the hypocritical self-presentation of others; it can also be costly for those who have been socialized or educated to overestimate their abilities. For not only will they sooner or later have to face the disappointing truth of their ordinariness, but they will not be in a nurturing or supportive environment when that happens; nor will they have built up the resilience that helps us survive and learn from those occasions when we discover our weaknesses and inadequacies.

There is sometimes pressure on us to be hypocritical from without; to say it *not quite* as it really is. Should this be in a good cause – so that others benefit, or to keep the social and organizational wheels turning – then we accept and even praise it. Should it be in order to create a deliberately misleading impression of ourselves, then we deprecate it. But do we also generate internal pressure that drives our own hypocrisy? Well, yes we do. And we do it by having moral and spiritual aspirations that are somewhat beyond our reach. This is necessary if we are not to be complacent. A moral aspiration is nothing if it is not something different to what we already truly are. Judith Shklar considers the mismatch that necessarily exists between aspiration and achievement by discussing the Victorian middle classes, who were subjected to a hail of criticism by the likes of Dickens, Carlyle, Mill and so on. Such critics articulated 'an enormous nausea at such a mass of insincerity, dishonesty, sentimentality, and wilful self-deception. Failure to face the facts and religious and moral pretence were blended in their eyes to form a single mass of hypocrisy.' Shklar recognizes that there is something wrong here, but does not see it as hypocrisy, since 'To fail in one's own aspirations is not hypocrisy.' The ethos of the Victorian middles classes involved no distance between what they said they believed in and what they sought to achieve. Their only hypocrisy, she argues, was in their complacency. 'They were hypocrites because they hid something evil when it was in their interest to do so.'

Shklar goes on to expand the distance between hypocrisy and self-hatred, and exonerates the Victorian middle classes of the extent of hypocrisy that their critics imputed to them. That doesn't in itself save or redeem them; not to have one vice is no guarantee of not having another, and hypocrisy may in fact not be the worst of vices at all – even if it is annoying and odious when we come across it in others. And it can certainly be genuinely annoying to witness a pompous ass telling everyone how they fully intend to become a better person. But it's not the intention itself that's annoying. It's the insincerity and the lack of self-awareness, coupled in this case with the emotional ignorance of not realizing how annoying one is being; but in the pompous ass this is probably an already settled trait.

But what does it mean – I return to my question again – to judge myself to be a hypocrite? Is this something I can ever sensibly do without giving up on that necessary tension that comes from being both self-aware and having spiritual aspirations? Is it not the case, in other words, that a sense of hypocrisy is in fact a by-product of virtue rather than evidence of vice? Shklar speaks of the 'self-hatred that marks all puritanism', and that does seem to be the greater risk. That we dislike, diminish or despise ourselves to the extent to which we honestly appraise the difference between our real self and our ideal or aspiring self. There is a dangerous line of thought to avoid here, however, and it is this. Given that there is often nothing much that we can do about our own inner reality (the dark side of the soul is, after all, *dark*), the easiest way not to be a hypocrite is to drop our social, moral and spiritual aspirations. If you don't even want to be a good person no one can call you a hypocrite for not being one. This is just the sort of muddle we get into if we think that hypocrisy is not only a simple vice but the worst one. Such, alas, is the sort of mistake we might well be inclined to make in today's moral climate, which makes unrealistic assumptions about the possibility of complete integrity and simplicity.

Despite the very bad press that hypocrisy has had since the time of the New Testament, it is *not* the vice of vices that we might at first think it is, either when we see it in others or perceive it in the tension between aspects of what we think, say and do. It is often when we *feel* hypocritical that we are in fact making some moral and spiritual progress. It follows that part of our spiritual journey is to learn how to live with the self-accusation of hypocrisy, the feeling of being a hypocrite. But while we have to learn how to cope with this we also have to continue to be moved by it and not to acquiesce complacently in it. When we feel that we are hypocritical it is important that we seek to overcome the feeling in the right way and for the right reasons. And the right reasons cannot be fear of being exposed as a hypocrite any more than they can be a desire to be a person of perfect motive and morals and complete and entire integrity. Certainly we fail if we acquiesce in the habits, attitudes and actions that are most dissonant with our moral and spiritual aspirations and in what we more or less knowingly project as our self-image. But we fail more profoundly if we give up on our ideals, or become defensive against the evidence of our dissonance, and end up losing that piquancy of self-awareness that prods us not to self-hatred but to repentance and reform, even while we know that it is part of our lot to remain a disappointment to ourselves, and to appear in the eyes of some to be at least something of a hypocrite.

Defensiveness

'Defensiveness' is resistance to the truth, to put it abstractly, or resistance to reality, to put it more concretely. It is the failure to acknowledge things that are not pleasing or congenial to us, whether it is a truth about ourselves, or the reality that the fantasy that we hold about the world or about other people, or another person, is not founded in fact. It is what we just won't see, what we can't hear, what we refuse to accept. Defensiveness is the abstract word that describes the darkness of the dark side of the soul. The metaphor works quite well because while the dark side sometimes gets a little brighter and sometimes a little murkier, so our defences come and go according to circumstance.

One question, then, is what makes us more or less defensive. Under what conditions do we most actively resist the truth, and under which do we most readily accept it? This is, when you come to think of it, a surprisingly important question, provided, that is, that you esteem and value the truth, at least in theory. And many of us do. Jesus said, 'the truth will make you free' and when in South Africa they had a 'Truth and Reconciliation Commission' the slogan was that 'truth is the road to reconciliation'. Not everyone thought so, of course. There were those who thought that the best way to let bygones be bygones was simply to draw a line under the horrors of the past and move on. The desire to draw such lines is a common one across the range of human affairs from the mildly embarrassing to the absolutely atrocious. This is close to the species of defensiveness that we might call 'denial'. Yet there is a big difference between those who say that something never happened and those who say that they don't want to hear any more about what happened or why.

When we talk about defensiveness, what is on our mind is the resistance to the psychic pain of confronting the truth. This is the truth that 'hurts'. It costs us very little to learn that hydrogen is the smallest atom, or that the moon is 239,000 miles from the earth. The fact that we have just offered a rather dismal performance on the tennis court or sung a note out of tune, or bored the Rotary Club to never previously seen levels of somnolence with our carefully prepared PowerPoint presentation, or just lost a contract because the financial information didn't add up, or have just driven through a red traffic signal because our attention wandered, are all much more difficult truths to accept. They do hurt, and that seems like the bad news. The good news, or so it may suddenly feel to us, is that they are contestable ('No! It was still amber!') or at least excusable ('I was very rushed in putting those figures together because someone in another office didn't supply the data on time') or can be relativized ('I have heard that they *always* fall asleep in the after-dinner talks'). Thus we excuse ourselves, or contest the observation, not in the interests of establishing the truth, but to save our reputation.

Or to be a touch more accurate, we do all this to save our *self-reputation*, our own view of ourselves, because no one else is at all convinced by such nonsense. The only person we fool when we are in defensive mode is ourselves. The others – friends, random observers, the police officer who is breathalysing us – are given no psychic pain whatsoever when they become aware of our imperfections and mistakes and errors; nor are they in any way shocked to observe our less than thorough excellence or utter brilliance. For them, the truth about us is both more nuanced and less disappointing. They see us as we really are because our failures and shortcomings are no more taxing to their nerves than the chemical formula of hydrogen or the distance from the earth to the moon. As far as they are concerned we are just another person and like everyone else they have ever met, we too have plenty of faults and failings. The only person who is not allowed to have such feet of clay is, paradoxically, the person whose faults and failings we are most familiar with. That is, me, I, myself.

Defensiveness has its primary reference with regard to truths about ourselves. We are at our most defended when we are resisting an element of self-awareness that we do not desire. It is our defended-ness that keeps our level of shame bearable, and in that regard it is perhaps a good thing, an act of kindness to ourselves which preserves our social functioning, our value to others, and our utility in the community. We are no good at all if we are paralysed by guilt, overcome with regret or remorse, or if we die of shame; and we can only bear so much of these burdens.

As we have seen with other vices, it's not so much a question of whether we have the vice or not, but of the extent, the awareness and the acknowledgement. It's not a question of whether we are defended or not, but whether we are excessively defended. This is not only a difficult question to answer from our own resources, but almost certainly an impossible one, for if our defence mechanisms are worth their salt they will not be under our conscious direction. This is not 'look away now' territory. It is the necessary matter of not taking on board everything that successfully enters our sensory organs. Humankind knows in its bones that it cannot bear much reality.

To take the pressure off ourselves for a moment (don't worry, it will soon return) we might want to consider whether our cultural environment encourages defensiveness, or whether it tends to encourage and enable us to accept the truth and take responsibility. This is a question about moral and spiritual authority. It is widely said that ours is a narcissistic society, encouraging uncritical and self-flattering self-regard, and to this is added the idea that we assume, compared with our forebears, extraordinarily high levels of *entitlement*. If this sort of analysis is anything like correct then we should perhaps be drawn in the direction of concluding that we are being encouraged by our cultural and social context to be defensive because our sense of personal responsibility is being eroded. Of course, our defensiveness can be encouraged by quite different dynamics too. For instance, if criticism is too frequent, or too harsh, or too shrill, or just plain unreasonable, we will seek ways of screening it out. Such defensiveness may in fact be conscious, or even the product of determined hard work. I have more than once advised people to try to screen out some of the hostile feedback they were getting from others. For while people can be calmly objective about the disappointing truths about us, they can also be mean and spiteful, and will sometimes take an opportunity to have a go at us quite unfairly, or to have a dig at our weaknesses or sore points, or to exploit our vulnerabilities. It is not a sin to turn a blind eye or deaf ear to such things. This is the good defensiveness of the cricketer who plays a cunning delivery with soft hands, taking the speed and ferocity out of the ball; not the bad defensiveness of the cricketer who refuses to accept what is obvious to everyone else – that the ball that hit the pad was on a collision course with the middle stump.

While it is helpful to see that a wide range of different truths might prompt our defensiveness to become maladaptively vigilant, and to note that we can do very little to make ourselves less defensive, as most of our defensiveness is necessarily below the level of our conscious awareness, this doesn't mean that there is nothing we can do about this vice. The most obvious thing is actively to seek objective feedback from the sort of person who is likely, indeed may be precisely commissioned, to say the sort of things that, while true, are just those things that we don't want to hear said. Exercises in 360-degree feedback, especially if mediated by someone who is keenly perceptive and tactful in their honesty, can present truths which even those who feel themselves to be more than averagely self-aware will find surprising, if not humbling and shaming. The sort of feedback that really works is that which seems to the recipient to have come to the wrong person. Why? Not because the recipient is especially bad, but because the feedback will have brought to light things from the darkest corners of the dark side of the soul. Such sudden shocks in self-awareness need to be handled with great care, and can be occasioned not only by this sort of intervention but by life changes, such as living with a new partner, the birth of a child, or moving to university. Experiencing an alien culture can also shock us into deeper self-understanding.

What is essential in all this, however, is to recognize that no one is perfect, not even you or me, and that our imperfections are not, contrary to what we sometimes feel, the things that are most before our eyes and on our minds, but those aspects of ourselves which are most hidden from us. That's a scary thought, that I am defending myself very adequately against the worst of my faults, failings, shortcomings, weaknesses and inadequacies, not to mention my nastiness, and that I am not aware of the worst aspects of myself. Maybe this is not true of absolutely everyone; the abject, as we saw in the last chapter, suffer from a different syndrome. But defensiveness is not only a fault of the arrogant or highly conceited. It is another 'ordinary vice' or 'everyday sin', and as such we need to find a way of accepting it without acquiescing to it or becoming complacent in our state of semi-self-awareness.

Certainty

One of the questions that haunts Mary Midgely's book *Wickedness* is whether or not people who do wicked or evil things intend to do wicked or evil things. She goes back to Aristotle, who, like Plato before him, believed that whereas we are aware of our weaknesses, our 'vice is unconscious'. She also refers to people whom she described as 'contentedly vicious'; that is, those who are untroubled by the harm or havoc they inflict. She notes that they 'do not as a rule describe themselves as vicious, nor even think of their actions as wrong'.

This is a very troubling observation, especially to those who do *not* think of themselves as especially bad, malicious or in any way vicious. If, typically, people don't know, or are not aware, when they are acting viciously and hurting others, then those of us who believe ourselves to be largely blameless find ourselves in a complex moral and spiritual predicament. Our confidence about our moral uprightness and probity is something that we should doubt and question. If people don't know what they are doing is as wrong as it is then (a) the whole question of remorse is even more complicated than we normally suppose and (b) we might one day wake up to find that we ourselves are perpetrators of evil not only worse than we had intended, but also beyond the worst reaches of our imagination. In response, we recall the child we once were, trying to cope with our accusing parent, teacher or friend by protesting that 'I didn't mean to', and remember just how harsh we thought it was that our excuse was not accepted. That something was broken, or a word or action judged to be hurtful, cruel, negligent, or merely 'very naughty', seems to bear no relation to what we were thinking of at the time. We had no idea that we were going to be judged for *this*. And just as wrong is wrong when you are child, so wicked is wicked when you are an adult, and evil is evil when you are a grown-up. That's what responsible maturity means. As Alexander Solzhenitsyn realized, when reviewing his life in the Gulag, 'In my most evil moments I was convinced that I was doing good, and I was well supplied with systematic arguments.'

It is unsettling to think that our solid conviction that we are doing good may one day be shown to be misplaced. One hundred per cent certainty is just such a pleasant experience. Such occasions come to us all, and they can be among life's more pleasurable and seductive moments. To be able to act with confidence, knowing that everything has been thought through, planned, measured, determined and so on; to engage in an activity without any doubt in the back of your mind, without the voice of either conscience or insecurity jabbering away, 'I'm really not so sure about this' – such are the moments of happy dreams. You marry the absolutely right person. You buy the best house. You opt for the perfect job – it wouldn't suit everyone, but it's clearly made for you. These are some of life's more golden days. 'I have never been more certain of anything,' we boast, before we realize, sometime later, that our certainty was not as wisely based as we thought at the time.

To draw attention to the pleasure of certainty is simultaneously to flag up its dangers. This is now a familiar theme in our exploration of how the vices work in us. It is not to knock the pleasure, but it *is* to say that we should drink it in responsibly, and try to be considerate to those around us when our personally pleasurable intoxication can have anti-social consequences. Our certainty is a danger not only to us but also to those around us, and to those whom we may, whether we realize it or not, impact and influence.

This suggests that certainty is in some ways like a drug. Certainty takes the edge off the keenness of our intellect, dulls us to emotional pain and has an addictive quality. Life is easier when we are drugged, and so we take another pill, have another shot, inject ourselves once more. Certainty can work like this, especially in a cultural environment where there is an overwhelming abundance of choice. It is in such a context that certainty becomes a rare commodity, a scarce good, so that when we one day feel the whoosh of hormones and the flashing of neurons in the pleasure-perceiving parts of the brain we are very agreeably overpowered.

The pleasures of certainty are not so great in traditional communities, or under authoritarian regimes, however. Here certainty becomes predictability and external control. The very fact that we know what's going to happen next and how the story will end is all very well when we are re-reading our favourite novel or watching an old film, but it's not what we want to happen in our own unfolding life story. No, the important thing here is that the story has an author, and that the person with the pen in hand, or with fingers tapping away at the keyboard of life, is me. Nonetheless, the charms of certainty do run deep. It is not uncommon for those who have recently been liberated from past oppression to look back to the 'good old days' of despotic rule and say, 'at least you knew where you were'. There is a deep-seated need in human beings for order and predictability, whereas anarchy and chaos are very bad environments not only for social and criminal justice but also for personal peace and flourishing. We are in 'but at least the trains ran on time' territory here, and nostalgia for the clip round the ear from the local police constable or the headmaster's use of the cane. One of the sadnesses of the latter, in my experience, was that it was usually pretty obvious who was going to end up getting the thrashing. It was definitely highly predictable, even to us kids, if not absolutely certain. Those all too audible smacks and yelps did their job, and made make you think 'that could be me'. But mostly the boys who were 'given the ruler' (girls were spared this in those unequal days) were those who had been beaten before, recidivism at school, just as in the wider world, being one of life's stronger certainties.

So – can this be serious? Is certainty really a sin, a vice? It's not in any of the traditional lists, but maybe that's because the list isn't long enough. Some certainty is excellent, and complete certainty in some areas of life is exactly what we would hope for. Even if we are rarely in the land of 100 per cent, we want to be up there in the high nineties when we put the key in the ignition of the car, or step out on the pavement when we believe the traffic to be halted by a red light. We want to be as certain as we can be that our dentist really is trained and experienced – and kind – and is not a psychopath who has been teeing up over recent years for one mad moment of mayhem which, as it happens, is going to coincide with my first check-up in a decade. And when we make life's big decisions we want to be confident that we are doing the right thing. But how confident is good and realistic and true? Someone may have done a scientific study on the correlation between 'wedding-day confidence that this relationship will last' and the 'length of the marriage'. My hunch is that it might not be very high, for there is something that feels a little bit defensive about certainty. Just as no person is perfect, so no relationship is guaranteed to succeed. That's part of the fun, excitement, point and purpose of life. It's not that we can prepare properly and then be certain that all will have a good time. It's that we prepare provisionally, and then have to make the best of what actually happens when, as it were, our little boat sails away from the safety of the harbour.

To learn that life is *not* about knowing what is going to happen next, but about being prepared and able to respond to the unexpected, is to take a step in the direction of practical and positive wisdom. Knowing that nothing much is certain is intrinsic to this. It's not that the desire for certainty is wrong. It's that it can easily be misplaced or pandered to. When we indulge our desire for certainty we distort our perception of reality. In much of life the best meaning of the word 'certainty' is something like, 'as confident as I can be after having pondered the matter carefully', or, 'actually I am not really sure, and I am churning away inside, but this is where I am going to put my faith and trust'. And thus we still walk to the dentist's chair, or to the podium to sing our solo, or into the interview room, or in front of our class of seven-year-olds on our first day as a teacher. Not certain, but well prepared and with trust that we will somehow be able to cope when the unexpected happens.

Perfectionism

Perfectionism is connected to vanity and the various species of bad pride that I have categorized as sins of vicious-regard. But I think it is more fundamentally a vice that reflects an impossible dream, an unachievable ideal. The main problem with perfectionism is that it offers a distorted vision of integrity. True integrity refers to the actual wholeness to which a human being may realistically aspire. It is liveable, inhabitable and above all possible; realistic, one might say. Perfectionism suggests that integrity comes from getting everything right. It is an archetypal impossible ideal – and an increasingly common and destructive one.

Perfectionism is one of the problems that afflict the narcissistic, and narcissism has become big business, or at least a big enterprise, in today's world. An interesting study analysed the vocabulary of fiction written since 1800 and concluded that our language is more self-referential than ever. This cultural background is perhaps the tip of the narcissistic iceberg, and a relatively benign one at that. Indeed, there are some positive aspects to narcissism, especially among the oppressed – provided that they have a good analysis of what really is oppressing them. It's no good a narcissistic teenager going into battle against their parents when the parents are just as oppressed as they are by pernicious social and political forces. Narcissism is helpful when those who are not treated with proper dignity and respect say, 'I am worth more than that', and find a good and constructive way forward. When a culture or subculture encourages people to be abject then injecting some narcissism into the system can be a helpful corrective.

But only up to a point.

Too much narcissism is very bad news, both for the narcissist him or herself, and for those he or she lives with. Especially when things go wrong, and in particular when, despite the splendid defences that narcissists build up, the truth breaks through and the narcissist discovers that they are in fact *not* perfect. Like many things in life, while this is not an absolute certainty, it is often simply a matter of time.

In recent years narcissism has become a recognized 'Personality Disorder' – at least in the United States. These are the features:

- Having an exaggerated sense of self-importance.

- Expecting to be recognized as superior even without achievements that warrant it.

- Exaggerating your achievements and talents.

- Being preoccupied with fantasies about success, power, brilliance, beauty or the perfect mate.

- Believing that you are superior and can only be understood by or associate with equally special people.

- Requiring constant admiration.

- Having a sense of entitlement.

- Expecting special favours and unquestioning compliance with your expectations.

- Taking advantage of others to get what you want.

- Having an inability or unwillingness to recognize the needs and feelings of others.

- Being envious of others and believing others envy you.

- Behaving in an arrogant or haughty manner.

Recognizable? Yes. Attractive? No. Do you recognize any of this in others? Yes? Well, think twice before you mention it, because part of the package is not responding well to criticism. Sentences like, 'Do you mind me saying that I think you are a bit of a narcissist?' do not have a very good chance of unfolding into a helpful conversation. Advanced-level tact is needed if you are to negotiate with a narcissist; that, or a degree in 'just putting up with it' – which is what used to happen around 'great men'. But that was in the days before our ambient level of narcissism had increased, and so it is less likely now than a few decades ago. Narcissists may be thicker on the ground these days, but unless they manage to isolate themselves by economic, political or religious power, they are likely to have quite a hard time. We are less tolerant of at least certain kinds of narcissism. That is why medical advice is available to those who suffer from the disorder – for when the fantasy of their own perfection is punctured, then the whole house of cards begins to collapse, and deep depression can unfold. These sad, chronically self-critical narcissists didn't imagine the possibly of themselves being wrong, or mistaken, or second-best. They certainly would not have been exploring, or even imagining, the dark side of the soul, for their desires were bound to be good and worthy and noble, simply by virtue of being *their* desires.

This is clearly bad news for narcissists, before or after tumbling to the truth of their imperfection. But are there any 'notes to self' to come out of this quick excursion to the place where people think that they are perfect?

As narcissism is a recognized personality disorder, there is such a thing as a 'narcissism test'. In fact there are quite a few online narcissism quizzes. Some of the questions seem a bit obvious – decide between 'I believe I am an exceptional person' and 'I believe I have a lot to learn from others', but perhaps people with average or high levels of narcissism, those who would probably be interested in doing such a test, would in fact expect to do rather well on it and

score high marks, not realizing that high narcissism is not something
of which to be proud . . .

Perfectionism is the vice most connected with the personality trait
or disorder of narcissism. It is a corruption of the good value of seeking
to have the best aims and objectives and fulfilling them to the best of
your ability. Aim for the sun and you might reach the moon, they say.
Such ideas make no sense to the perfectionist, who wouldn't be able to
celebrate the lesser, but nonetheless remarkable, achievement because
all they would notice is their own emotional reaction to having failed
to reach the sun. Perfectionism dooms one to disappointment, even
highly successful disappointment (an especially sad state of mind), just
as narcissism dooms one to the dawning of the day when the younger,
brighter star appears on the horizon and a crucial aspect of self-respect
or even identity is lost. Silver medals are wonderful achievements and
genuine sources of pride – unless you are a narcissistic perfectionist.

Bruno Bettelheim long ago came up with the solution to
perfectionism. It is the idea of being 'good enough'. This is especially
important in the realm of human relationships. Bettelheim's most
famous book was about parenting, *The Good Enough Parent*. If
anyone has the energy to put pen to paper, there is scope for a series
of similar books – 'Good Enough Manager', 'Good Enough Spouse',
'Good Enough Gardener', not to mention the 'Good Enough Painter',
'Good Enough Pianist', 'Good Enough Writer', and so on. Such books
are of no use to the very rare geniuses who will achieve unbelievable
standards of technical perfection, or artistic works of unimaginable
creativity. We should be glad that no one ever counselled Mozart or
Van Gogh to be 'good enough'. But they paid dearly for their self-
belief, and no society or community could be happily based on

such relentless singularity. For most of us, most of the time, in most societies and for most purposes good enough is just perfect.

Perfect integrity is not simple. It's simply impossible. True integrity is something much messier, and is undermined not by the truth of who we are, but by the impossible dreams and vain fantasies that led us to be too hard on hypocrisy, excessive in defensiveness, naïve in our certainty, and dangerously unrealistic in our narcissism.

Perfectionism, like the other vices considered in this chapter, is a sin against the truth of who we are that unnecessarily besmirches our actual, good enough but nonetheless flawed, incomplete, and inconsistent integrity.

6

Temporal Disjunctions

All sins are negative, but some perhaps are more negative than others. Evagrius believed that the noonday demon was the most pernicious of all, and he called it 'acedia', using a Greek word that was the negative of 'care'. The one-word translation of this is 'sloth' but, as several writers have recognized, 'sloth' doesn't really carry the full weight or range of the word, or communicate the astonishing power of the noonday demon. 'Careless' is nearer the mark, but even that is a weak-sounding word. Maybe acedia could be idiomatically translated, 'Don't care!' or 'Not bothered'. Certainly there is something far more important and insidious in acedia than the words 'sloth' or 'laziness' suggest. It's not just the matter of failing to make enough effort. It's an attitude that suggests that making an effort is a mistake, or, to put it slightly differently, a mood in which effort is pointless because life itself has become disenchanted, or has lost its meaning.

Solomon Schimmel, a professor of Jewish education and psychology and a psychotherapist, does use the word 'sloth' in his book *The Seven Deadly Sins* and brings to it an unusual perspective, taking a particular interest in the patterns of thought that might lead us into its tentacles. Looking at sloth today, he connects it with the modernist vocabulary – 'anomie', 'despair' and 'depression'. Considering it historically, he also connects it with words like 'aridity' or 'dryness' that mystics and others used to describe the times when they found themselves disinclined to pray, or were just not interested in God. Such spiritual aridity and disenchantment with life does not depend for its disappointing reality on holding a faith and feeling it go cold. It can happen with any activity that was once absorbing and delightful. The feeling that what was once rewarding and a source of delight and wonder is now just a matter of going through the motions is well known today to plenty of people whose mindset is secular. But we should distinguish several forms. There is the episodic dullness and disappointment that is part of a genuinely difficult yet potentially creative or transformative process. This is acedia that will pass, though it seems as if it won't. Then there is the chronic disillusion and forlorn despair that might be a form of burnout or depression.

In her searingly insightful and honest memoir, *Acedia and Me*, Kathleen Norris explores the social and medical complexity of her own experience of acedia. Her starting point is that far from being the *noonday* demon, acedia is on hand at any hour of the day or night for 'anyone whose work requires self-motivation and solitude, anyone who remains married "for better or worse", anyone who is determined to stay true to a commitment that is sorely tested in everyday life'. She considers writers as diverse as Søren Kierkegaard – who saw acedia as the 'silent despair' of which his father spoke – and Bertrand Russell who, at the age of fourteen, could not bear the prospect of longevity. 'Acedia', she writes, 'contains within itself so many concepts:

weariness, despair, ennui, boredom, restlessness, impasse, futility.'
One of the twists she finds in St John of the Cross, the Spanish mystic
who wrote of 'the dark night of the soul', is that attempts to move
beyond the problem repeatedly fail, so that even desire to overcome
spiritual aridity dries up. And furthermore, the benighted soul begins
to fear that the darkness and difficulty is of its own making. The only
drops of water in the dryness are tears of self-recrimination and guilt
for a situation that has long been intractable.

Acedia certainly implies despondency and discontent. You could
think of it as a cousin of melancholy, or the sibling of depression,
suggestions that raise those difficult questions about cause and
attribution. It's one thing to talk poetically about demons, or
metaphorically about the dark side of the soul, but what if this is all
caused by a chemical imbalance in the brain? Antidepressants were
invented in the twentieth century and there are plenty of people who
now live functional and fulfilling lives because they take them. And
the use of artificial stimulants keeps many active during the long
working day or at the surge or dip in certain hormone cycles. We
might wonder whether Evagrius would have ever spoken about the
noonday demon if he had had an espresso machine in his hermitage
or a pharmacy around the corner.

The suggestion that chemicals might finally rob the noonday
demon of its power, however, fails to recognize the reality and
importance of experiences that we call apathy and boredom, as well
as more contemporary versions of it such as 'burnout syndrome'
or, my own particular suggestion, chronic busyness. Apathy is not
only a lack of excitement and enthusiasm, but also a disconnection
from concern and engagement. When we are apathetic we fail

to be moved by compassion or empathy, or to be animated by purpose. Boredom is a state or mood in which we find ourselves when presented with information that, for whatever reason, doesn't entertain or interest us, or the more settled condition that we experience when life seems not to have meaning. Both apathy and boredom are experienced as part of depression, but they also exist outside depression.

There is often something sad about acedia, and a historic note is pertinent to this. While Evagrius distinguished between 'sadness' and 'acedia', later compilers of lists tended to conflate the two. This is one reason why it is difficult to be precise about exactly what acedia is. But it's not only description and interpretation that make this difficult. The phenomena are difficult too, and also wide-ranging. And so we are unlikely to get to the bottom of the matter in the short space of this chapter. Nevertheless, our exploration of the dark side of the soul would be even less complete than it is if we did not bother to consider the darkness of acedia, which is not the mental illness of depression, but the negative attitude and mood for which we are responsible – a thoughtless, careless, dull and self-defeating spiritual and temporal dislocation.

One aspect of acedia that is not normally explored is the extent to which time is an important consideration. Manifestations and versions of acedia, I want to propose, are all characterized by a distortion of our relationship with time. They are all *temporal disjunctions*. This again takes us back to the roots of it all, the hermit Evagrius believing that the sun had stopped in the sky in the middle part of the day. And there is a contemporary twist in all this too. For while the word acedia is traditionally connected with heaviness and lethargy I want to suggest that it is absolutely caught up with what seems like the opposite. The relentless *busyness* that many people experience today. But first, let us turn our minds to the dreary subject of sloth.

Sloth

The idea that sloth is a sin has become a cause of mockery in recent years. This is perhaps not too surprising, given the frenetic pace of modern life, the overwhelming range of occasions for choice, and the superabundant flows of information that many are aware of experiencing today.

Taking the perspective that the prevailing sin of our time is not the failure to do enough, but the failure to slow down and stop from time to time, Wendy Wasserstein takes the opportunity given by being commissioned to write about sloth to write a mock self-help book, suggesting that sloth should be an aspiration, and offering all sorts of lessons in how to become more slothful, or, as she puts it, 'a sloth'.

Integral to Wasserstein's image of successful slothery is the goal of achieving 'lethargiosis', and she commends her 'Ten Rules of Sloth' as ways to help achieve this end. We need only scan the first five to get the idea.

1   Do not clean up.

2   Do not wash.

3   Learn to love yourself as you are.

4 Stop competing.

5 Food is no longer an issue.

The point of such 'rules of sloth' is not to help the adherent live a more balanced, contented and effective life, but to remove the motivation to do any kind of work, discharge any duty, or to seek to change anything that is wrong, harmful or unjust. Presented ironically as a path to a better life, it is clearly a path to inertia and apathy. Wasserstein writes that 'lethargiosis is not a state of tranquility, it is a state of pointlessness'. In her knowingly toxic scheme, meditation is unhelpful as it takes work and requires a 'tidy, methodical mind'. She concludes that 'the state of lethargiosis is not a trance but an enervated limp'. That enervated limp is an aspect of acedia. Let's take the easy option and call it sloth itself.

Simon Laham takes an un-ironic stance when he lampoons sloth in *The Joy of Sin*, saying that 'sloth' is innocuous, as it means, essentially, 'take it easy'. Laham believes that we have been ill-served by the religious traditions that have made us think that it is bad to rest. In particular, he blames 'the Protestants', saying that for them idleness was a great threat to their deep work ethic. He mentions that Bertrand Russell and Robert Louis Stevenson both wrote essays in praise of idleness.

Laham's peroration in favour of sloth refers to the importance of sleep, and argues that the wandering mind is often more purposeful than we realize. He tells us about various psychological experiments which show that hard work doesn't always pay off. For instance, we often make better judgements if we don't spend too much time and effort analysing things, and, perhaps more surprisingly, deliberation can even make our decisions less just. Laham also refers with approval to the slow cities or 'Cittaslow' movement in Italy, reporting research evidence which concludes that in cities where the pace of life is faster people are less kind and helpful to each other. In the end he grudgingly concludes that, 'As with other sins, sloth does have its drawbacks. Indulge in it too often and you'll never get anything done.' But he also believes that the tradition of calling it a sin blinds us to the positive side of sloth. 'Indulge in [sloth] appropriately and you'll be smarter and perhaps even a little more virtuous for your (lack of) effort.'

Informative and sympathetic as Laham is, he does not manage to deconstruct the suggestion that there is a vice properly called sloth, because, as we have seen, a vice is not something that is always evil, but something that is problematic or hostile to us under certain circumstances, in particular when it becomes a disproportionate part of our character. It is simply not slothful to have a good night's sleep, or to be careful not to confuse effort with effectiveness. For all her amusing slothery, Wasserstein *does* distinguish between tranquillity and lethargy; and it is lethargy that sloth takes us to, that itself being a parody of the appropriate use of rest, relaxation and refreshment that are part of a good and healthy life.

We are in the realm of effort here, and one thing that talking about laziness, sloth and the like helpfully requires of us is to be realistic about the value of effort. In a world where people describe their commitment in terms of making 110 per cent effort, it is helpful to be reminded of the Pareto Principle, which says that 80 per cent of our effectiveness comes from 20 per cent of our work. The message from this is not 'work harder' but 'work smarter'. It also helps to remember that when you plot stress against performance, the graph is a bell curve and suggests that the best results come not when people are making a huge effort but when they are in the middle of the effort-making range. This means that for many who are trying hard, improved performance will come not from trying harder still, but from relaxing a bit. This is not a vindication of the lazy. It remains the case that those who are not yet trying very hard at all will do better if they make more of an effort. The fundamental point, however, is that there is no one law for all people all the time – whether it is 'try harder' or 'take a rest'. These things depend on many factors, and so we need to develop the personal awareness that allows us to adjust and respond to the unfolding situations and circumstances of life as they go by.

A sensible question to ask here concerns where our inclinations lie. Are we naturally disposed to be indolent, or are we hyperactive? Are we more likely to say 'yes' when we should say 'no', or to say 'no' when we should say 'yes'? To come to a view about such things is to come to understand our weaknesses more fully. In the context of sloth this means that we need to think about things like the quality of our effort or the appropriateness of our activity level. It is therefore slothful not only to be lazy, or to skive, but also to be so busy as not to let others do their fair share. If you have ever heard anyone say, 'it's easier to do it myself' you will have heard sloth talking. The problem is that they have neglected to do the extra work of allowing others to participate and contribute. In the case where the others concerned are children who might by their participation and effort not only have had fun but also gained esteem and skill, this is a sad and serious matter. One might even call it abuse – abuse of the opportunity you have by your superior status to do things for others that they would be better doing for themselves.

The community-organizing pioneer Ed Chambers coined the phrase the 'iron rule' as an adaptation of the golden rule. Whereas the golden rule is to 'do unto others as you would like them to do to you', the iron rule says 'never, do for others what they can do for themselves'. This is his approach to the more familiar idea that sometimes it is kindness that kills – or at least harms or incapacitates others, robbing them of a potentially formative challenge. The oft-quoted maxim, 'Give a man a fish and you feed him for a day; teach him to fish and you feed him for a lifetime', works at home too. It is unusual to attribute our own well-meaning but gradually disempowering doing of good to sloth, and doubtless there are other vicious drivers too – such as the vainglorious desire to be seen to be the perfect parent – or at least the hyper-assiduous parent. And we do often admire those who do more than their fair share. But we should think again if this means that others are denied their fair share. Fairness is fairness – even when it comes to doing tiresome tasks.

Sloth is the origin of both 'thoughtlessness' and 'busyness'. On thoughtlessness, Mary Midgely's suggestion is that 'the harm that can be done by not thinking is literally immeasurable'. At first reading this seems quite paradoxical. There are worse things, it would seem, than being lazy and taking it easy. It is the busybodies who, by and large, make bad things happen. No one starts a war by sitting in a deck chair or having a lie-in. And yet in a quotation attributed to Edmund Burke and often repeated in various forms, 'all that is needed for evil to triumph is for good men to do nothing'.

Thoughtlessness underlies many of our sins of omission – the good things we somehow neglect. These include the things we forgot to do, or didn't get round to because we were preoccupied with the urgent, or the expedient, or the simply more congenial and attractive. This is the failure to answer the phone call that you suspect, but do not know, to be your ageing mother because you are absorbed in your hobby or some out-of-hours work. The second most likely area is perhaps to realize retrospectively that during the period of our neglect of something important, we were all along deceiving ourselves about the significance of what we were actually doing, and that our conscience was whispering away all the while, but that we ignored it. This is the failure to pick up the phone yourself and call your mother because there were always more urgent things to do. This awkward, unworthy and embarrassing semi-self-deception is a sad, but perhaps not uncommon condition. We might excuse ourselves for it because this is how we get though the working day and domestic evening. It's not really good but neither is it really bad – though on reflection it is, in fact, rather worse than we realized at the time. And that's one of the problems with thinking about it.

Sloth lies behind many such omissions and matters of neglect, yet people rarely do 'nothing'. What they actually do is 'something else', and it is when there are a lot of 'something elses' that are more compelling than tasks or actions that are in fact more important, pressing or noble, that it is appropriate to talk about busyness as a member of the acedia family. The more insidious vices often disguise themselves as virtues, and busyness offers a good case study of this. But before exploring that we must brace ourselves to think about boredom, or we will keep putting it off – and yes, prevarication is another aspect of acedia.

Boredom

Evagrius saw sloth – or acedia – as the 'noonday demon'. He famously wrote that it attacks 'the monk about the fourth hour [viz. 10 a.m.] and besieges his soul until the eighth hour [viz. 2 p.m.]. First of all, he makes it appear that the sun moves slowly or not at all, and that the day seems to be fifty hours long.' This reminds me of a lecture that I attended in my first year at university where I was not alone in feeling that the clock had stopped at ten past ten in the morning. Naturally I didn't blame myself, or for that matter really believe that the clock had stopped. The problem was the boring lecturer. For us, he seemed to be a mid-morning demon.

Part of the experience of boredom is to look for causes outside ourselves. We are cross and irritated when bored, and are far too listless to want to take responsibility for our negativity. Feeling that the sun or clock has stopped, we don't feel the ecstasy of timelessness, but feel rather that we are trapped in futility; all sense of a positive future has gone, hope is eclipsed. There is lethargy here, and a growing sense that time itself is so slow as to be painful; the present moment has become a torture chamber for the soul. The Norwegian philosopher Lars Svendsen writes that, 'In boredom, time becomes "refectory" because it will not pass like it usually does . . .'

No one ever aims to be bored. Boredom is something that happens to us when we don't have any aims, and which we then resent. In this way it is different to frustration. Boredom is based on passivity and makes us yet more passive. This is the vicious circle of boredom, the sad spiral of sloth. Svendsen suggests that one of the features of boredom is that it is 'a mood that is reminiscent of an absence of moods', a kind of 'non-mood' that prevents us relating to things. Boredom is therefore, as we all know, connected to loneliness. Not the absence of others but the inability to relate with them. The problem is that we don't then address the cause of our boredom; rather, we let it bear fruit in unhelpful attitudes and actions and we are trapped by its enervated pointlessness into an experience of hopelessness.

And so we want out. This is the strange thing about boredom. It is not at all like the contented dawdling on things that is refreshing, or idling in ways that are pleasurable. It's not 'taking your time', or 'taking it easy'. It is certainly not to 'take care'. Boredom creates a fear of time and leads to distraction, dissipation and unrewarding, unhelpful, aimless activity or, on another occasion, desireless inactivity. The range and variety of ways out of boredom that people devise is impressive, one of the increasingly popular being fame. We mentioned Andy Warhol in this context earlier – a man for whom boredom was a key concept in his pursuit of nothingness. For him the famous fifteen minutes of fame would be seen to be significant not because it involved giving recognition or honour where it was due, but because the fame itself is *imagined* to be worthwhile. In this he was genuinely prescient.

Broadly speaking there are two different types of boredom. The first is situational boredom – that's Evagrius in the afternoon, me in the lecture, and you in a traffic jam or, if you are especially unlucky, at work, or if you are unwise, channel surfing on TV. This is the boredom caused by our failure to find anything of interest in what we are experiencing or encountering at the time. Sometimes particular individuals are boring to us. We simply do not share a common interest or we find their remarks to be banal. This is all 'situational boredom'.

The other kind of boredom is more generic and sometimes called 'existential'. This is not the situation in which you find that things leave you cold and unmoved, but a disposition or perspective in which everything appears to be pointless and without meaning. This is the boredom of Andy Warhol and Samuel Beckett. It is 'Waiting for Godot' although you know that Godot will never come, believing in the importance of a 'Moment' that is relentlessly postponed. Heidegger called this being bored with boredom. There is no possibility of interest or meaning. This is a life of relentless lightness. Even your own self is a matter of complete disinterest and indifference to you.

One doesn't need to be a theorist of boredom to know its effects or to be challenged to deal well with them. Nor does one need to be placed in a trapped situation and subjected to a monologue to experience its enervating anguish. One arena where I experience something that I think could be described as boredom is the supermarket, where I am presented with more choices than I could ever number, never mind evaluate. Let me call this 'supermarket acedia', and warn you about meeting the mid-aisle demon. The supermarket is emotionally and spiritually a dangerous place to be unless you have either (a) a list of exactly what to get that was drawn up in advance and that clarifies which of the various forms of the product you need to buy; or (b) a good deal of personal experience of dealing with supermarkets and a clear strategy for making decisions; or, preferably, (c) a companion who is in possession of either that list or who has the skills and experience to thrive in this situation.

Supermarkets are spiritually dangerous, at least to some frail souls. It is the opposite of a wilderness, but still it is a place for acedia to strike.

Boredom is not so much bad in its own right as dangerous. The bored person is vulnerable to being led astray, or to allowing their minds to create destructive diversions for themselves. This is not to judge those who have become listless or bored, but to recognize that we are all the same in this regard. It is to say that not only is boredom a painful experience and a trial, but it can also be the beginning of trouble. This is one reason why institutions such as schools, especially residential schools, create very full timetables and make life rich and interesting and engaging for their students. This strategy goes back to St Benedict, who realized that the spiritual life of hermits was too difficult and dangerous for most people and that without structure and community they would be prey to acedia and, once listless and dispirited, would be led astray into restless, self-indulgent but nonetheless hopeless and un-caring aimlessness.

Those who seek to prevent trouble by organizing the lives of others are following the lead of St Benedict with his rule of structure, order and accountability. Such words – structure, order and accountability – do not have a very exciting ring to them. They are dull, and to many people they may well come across as 'boring', but it is limitless freedom, together with lack of accountability and purpose, that make for real boredom. That's why people get bored in a dull lecture at university or if unemployed, but not if working hard on a building site. One needs time to be bored – it comes with leisure. And so it comes, sooner or later, to spoil our holiday. Holiday boredom is an experience that, if mild but sharp enough, can be a helpful part of the recreation and refreshment necessary for a positive return to our normal routines.

But the holiday dip in energy is boredom within a limiting structure. Boredom without that sort of structure is a different matter.

Boredom is the vice that afflicts people both when there are too many constraints and when there are too few. We can call the first situational and the second existential – but from the inside boredom is boredom, a kind of hell on earth. It is a strange hell. Those who are suffering pain or persecution do not usually think of themselves as bored, nor do those who are in a place of physical danger, whether exposed to the elements or to human violence. In particular, the very hungry don't complain of boredom; they complain of being hungry. Boredom is an affliction of the reasonably comfortable. There is even a hint of nausea or disgust, or maybe self-disgust, in the experience of boredom. This is connected with the everyday expression, 'I'm fed up'. The bored won't describe themselves as 'reasonably comfortable'; they will be aware not of what they have, but of what they lack. But that awareness will be vague and unfocused.

What do you want?
'I don't know.'
When do you want it?
'Very soon.'

This might be the protest cry of the bored. And it could continue.

Why do you want it?
'I don't know.'
How will you feel when you get it?
'Fine for a while and then much the same again soon after, I'm afraid.'

Boredom is connected both to being sated and not being sated. It's not only 'not bothered' but also 'full, but not satisfied'. Insatiability, which we will consider in connection with avarice, is closely connected. 'Fed up' is about it.

Once boredom sets in, the bored repeatedly fail to act wisely. They find it difficult, if not impossible, to know what to do because boredom has robbed them of their sense of purpose and direction. The bored are people whose unthought-through efforts in the end let them down. Thereby they prove to themselves the futility of action and the truth that life is, well, boring and pointless. Boredom is a vicious circle indeed. When it traps us, the demon of sloth sleeps soundly. But we don't necessarily remain sloths ourselves. Boredom may seem to be endlessly enduring, but we do from time to time surface from it – the sun hadn't actually stopped in the sky or the clock at ten past ten. But once bitten, twice shy. The experience of boredom strikes a double fear in us. Fear of constraint, being caught in boring company or stuck with a boring task, but also fear of freedom, in the form of extended periods of time without constraint. And these two paradoxically connected fears can easily drive us to one of the most startling contemporary forms of acedia: busyness.

Busyness

Boredom doesn't make us busy, but fear of boredom might. So too might avarice or anxiety. For busyness is not today simply the way we respond to a set of demands where more than usual is required of us; it has become a way of life, a new norm and even an occasion of boasting, or as someone has put it, busyness is often a boast disguised as a complaint.

We have seen already that in her book *Deadly Vices* Gabriele Taylor urges us to reconnect the noun and adjectival form of the word 'vice'. In this way she seeks to return the word 'vicious' to its correct meaning. So when Taylor says that something is vicious, she doesn't mean that it's like a hungry dog, but that it has the quality or nature of a vice. And so she speaks of the 'viciousness' of the deadly sins with sentences like 'what makes envy vicious . . .' Adopting this correct use of the word I want to propose that there is more than one form of busyness. There is 'virtuous busyness', and there is 'vicious busyness'. And it is vicious busyness that we are concerned with here.

Vicious busyness is the state we find ourselves in when we start using the word 'busy' both as a boast and as a complaint. It's what happens when we have fallen into the 'acceleration trap' of contemporary life. Busyness doesn't appear on the list of seven deadly sins, and is not usually discussed in the terms I am using here. Busy people are seen to be successful and admirable and yet as oppressed and downtrodden victims of pressures beyond themselves. When it is put like this, seasoned sin-spotters will immediately appreciate that there is something strange going on here in the realm of responsibility.

Vicious busyness is often performed busyness. It draws attention to itself with a range of behaviours such as quick movements, short sentences, darting glances (especially over the shoulder of the person who is talking to you), short attention span, limited peripheral vision, and self-importance. This is 'white-rabbit behaviour'. Many of these are symptoms of stress, and vicious busyness is in some ways a failure to deal with stress appropriately. But there's more to it than that. It's also got a strong narcissistic streak, which is why one of the antidotes to busyness is to remember that 'no one is indispensable, not even me'. But these are hard words for narcissists to own.

Both narcissism and vicious busyness are signs of our times. Life is speeding up and we speed up with it. Phrases like 'all in good time' fall out of use. Busyness is driven by the same change in values that overestimates the importance of fame. Just as the false value of 'fame' has replaced the true value of quality of achievement, so in the case of busyness it is the false assumption of urgency that has replaced the reality that there is often more time than we think to do what needs to be done. We all make mistakes in the way we prioritize, but the viciously busy have taken into themselves an engine that generates prioritizing mistake after prioritizing mistake on an industrial scale. And the basis of all those mistakes is thinking that time is a simple, linear and scarce resource. There are ways in which time is exactly that, and this sort of time, *chronos*, is the time by which efficiency is measured, the sort of time that according to Benjamin Franklin 'is money'.

There is a lot to be said for *chronos*. Without it none of those timetables that organizations and societies depend on would work, and, as we have seen, the old hermit Evagrius didn't like it at all when the sun seemed to stop in the sky. *Chronos* itself isn't vicious. But time becomes vicious, and we become viciously busy, when we treat time as if it were *only chronos*.

What is this life if, full of care,
We have no time to stand and stare?

The contemplative moment depends on there being other dimensions to time. One of these is *kairos*. This is timeliness, or 'opportunity time'. It is the time of the right moment. Religions recognize this in organizing prayer times and festivals. Secular society has traditionally done it in terms of organizing meals and holidays. The Sabbath, when kept in a traditional way, is an interruption of *chronos*, and makes little sense in terms of the relentless logic of *chronos* itself. But as the theologian Karl Barth said, 'there is no god called *chronos*'. To fall into busyness, on the other hand, is to act as if we believe that there is exactly such a god. Certainly there are obligations, duties and responsibilities that are marked in the diary or the calendar. But to treat a duty or obligation as something that scatters all other priorities to one side is to allow viciousness in – the sort of viciousness that is self-harming, other-harming and actually not a very sensible way of dealing with reality. Yes, there is an adrenaline rush, and a feeling of purpose and grandiosity, but these are manifestly hostile pleasures.

Or are they? And do I mean 'grandiosity'? Well, yes, because this is just a posh and archaic word for 'narcissism'. But sense of purpose? This actually gets to the heart of the matter. What is being criticized here is the sense of purpose that comes from a simple demand that is wrongly considered to be urgent. If we derive our sense of purpose from a distorted sense of urgency then we will soon find ourselves living in a way that depends for its overall sense of purpose on there being a crisis to attend to. This in turn leads the hungry human mind to seek and find more and more crises, and, when it doesn't find any, to connive to create them.

You don't find this convincing? A survey of 'time traps' has ranked 'management by crisis' as the top time trap in organizations on two separate occasions. The other leading causes have changed over the years but seeing a management team hop from crisis to crisis remains the major source of time poverty, urgency and busyness. *Chronos* may not be a god, but when we treat it as one we get into the very vicious circle of increasing stress and decreasing time. This is not good at all, and it is one of the reasons why this contemporary form of acedia needs to be named and shamed.

Just as a false and fabricated sense of purpose is the cause of much busyness, so a good, long-term and proper sense of purpose, one that acknowledges not only the demands of *chronos* but the opportunities of *kairos*, and takes into account the hope that we might both flourish as people and live together well as a global community, the ultimate 'common good', is precisely what we need in order to deal with vicious busyness.

Evagrius used the word 'acedia' to put a label on one particular distortion of his relationship with time. Over the years the word has been used, whether in its Greek form or in various translations, to refer to a number of related issues. In our own day it is appropriate to pick up the apparently benign word 'busy' or 'busyness' and give it the same treatment. This does not mean that all busyness is bad, but that there is a vicious form of busyness that is itself not something passing, but something chronic (itself derived from 'chronos'); not the product of a sudden change in events, but something that is demanded by pressures that have become normal; not something that we are well adapted to respond to, but something that depletes and erodes us in body, mind and spirit. This vicious busyness is less a product of actual physical need, and more a product of attitude and expectation that ultimately feeds on itself in an ever-accelerating spiral towards insignificance. All these are reasons *not* to describe yourself as busy. To do so is to say that you have fallen foul not of the noonday demon, but of the demon that never sleeps.

Nostalgia

What is nostalgia? The answer depends on who you ask and when you ask them. Back in the day it was a serious problem, but today the word evokes a 'warm fuzzy feeling' that takes us back in memory to a certain time in the past. Psychologists talk of a 'reminiscence bump' which accords with our late teens and early twenties. Ah, those were the days, and, as we know, whole tranches of the broadcasting industry are aimed at reconnecting older people with their nostalgia by offering them the music of 'their' era.

Nostalgia hasn't always been so benignly smiled upon, however. The word was created in the late seventeenth century to describe the attitude of Swiss mercenaries who were a long way from home and who would weep, refuse to eat and in some cases become suicidal. Nostalgia was at one time a registered psychiatric disorder, and has often been seen as a problem of immigrant communities and others who are 'home-sick'.

Looked at in this way, nostalgia is a melancholic longing for the past. There may be good emotional reasons for nostalgia – maybe we really were happier then, maybe the summers were more summery, the food tastier, the fun funnier. If the psychologists are right, however, our nostalgia is not for an actual golden age when things were better, but for a time of life when we were going through a lot of change, and laying down the memories that would become integral to our identities; not to mention making life choices – spouse, career, home – that would create the framework for our future lives. There could even be something adaptive about this. Looking back to the times when commitments were made and seeing them as good days might well have the positive consequence of inclining someone to try to deal constructively with the challenge of faithfulness and loyalty that may come in later years.

There is more to nostalgia than encouraging reminiscence, however. Quite young people can look back happily to the past. Children can be sticklers for adhering to what they understand to be 'tradition' or 'what we always do'. And some older people might take a less rose-tinted view of their formative years – not least if some of those major life decisions delivered real unhappiness. Nostalgia can take different forms – happy nostalgia, elegiac nostalgia, regretful nostalgia. And might it even be that remorse could be considered a kind of nostalgia? Longing for lost innocence rather than regretting the actions that caused it to be lost.

Nostalgia has various triggers. There are the involuntary ones like smell, the known ones like music, and the organized ones like photograph albums at the domestic level, and local history classes and archive offices on the more civic and social level.

Nostalgia is the enemy of those who want to lead organizations forward. 'But we have always done it this way' is the phrase any leader dreads hearing. The fact that it is almost certainly not true is beside the point. When people say this they are speaking from their nostalgic hearts. This is conservatism with a small 'c', and it informs Conservatism with a big 'C'. And there is some wisdom in it, just as there is wisdom in the desire for progressive politics. One says we should do better, the other says we could do worse. Naturally enough, those who see it one way will castigate those who see it the other way. Thus progressives will see traditionalists as stuck in the past (or the mud) and conservatives as regressive. Conservatives will see progressives as naïve and reckless, and traditionalists will believe that the proponents of change seek 'change for change's sake' or risk 'throwing the baby out with the bathwater'.

Clearly such discussion can, and will, go on and on. There are those who favour the past, and those who favour the future. That's one way of looking at it. Another is slightly different, and it involves asking the question, 'what are the legitimate and appropriate ethical and emotional claims of the past and the future, and how do they compare with those of the present moment?'

This sounds like a rather complicated question, and it is. But it is also a very important question, and it remains to be seen whether human beings are ever going to have the courage, confidence and creativity to give it the priority and space it needs in social and cultural life. It is a question for each person as to whether they have these qualities in sufficient strength to be able to address nostalgia at the personal and relational level, and to decide how much real time – how many present moments – it deserves.

One of the best-selling books in the spirituality genre is Eckhart Tolle's *The Power of Now*. A lot of it is about the weirdness of the present moment. If it has a serious challenger in the world of published spirituality today it comes from one of two related sources. One is the interest in 'Mindfulness' and the other is the recent and astonishing surge in colouring books for adults.

What all these have in common is an attempt to recapture the beauty, dignity, importance and priority of the present moment. Although all this is associated mostly with Buddhism it can equally well be seen as an application of Jesus' teaching in the Sermon on the Mount: 'Consider the lilies of the field . . .' And it is when we lose our connection with the present moment that our relationship with time becomes 'vicious' or 'sinful' in the sense that we have been using the words here. But our connection with the present moment is not to be found at the expense of a relationship with the past, or even at the expense of our relationship with the future. A good relationship with time gives all three their due.

Quite what this three-dimensional relationship looks like when it takes a virtuous form is not something that has been specifically and overtly addressed by the traditions that we have been considering here, though the question of a maladaptive or inappropriate relationship with time does run through and around the minds of the religious, the spiritual and those concerned with matters of mental health. A recent and overt contribution to this question has come from two psychologists at Stanford University who have developed the idea that we all have a distinctive 'time perspective'. Zimbardo and Boyd identify six different types of time perspective that we might, for all our idiosyncrasies, fall into, and these are, unsurprisingly, made up of relationships with the past, present or future.

All this may seem a very long way from poor old Evagrius getting into a torpor as the sun rose to its zenith in the sky, but it is fundamentally about the same stuff: how we relate to the passage of time without being drawn inappropriately (a) into the clutches of the past at the expense of the present and the future, (b) into the hedonistic or fatalistic dizziness of the present moment so that we forget both our identity and our responsibilities, or (c) into worrying about or planning or trying to control the future to the extent that we both forget all we have to be thankful for in the past, and miss the intriguing and intrinsically rewarding details of the many present moments of our lives.

It is a little unfair to call all this 'nostalgia', as the word really means inordinate love of the past, whereas what we have been briefly considering here includes this alongside relating badly to the future and to the present moment. There are no words for these vices that are temporal disjunctions, however, and so for now 'nostalgia' will have to do, and we must trust that in the fullness of time an acceptable neologism for the vice of not inhabiting time in an appropriate, healthy or responsible way will be formed, understood and accepted. When in the grip of such a vice we confuse and confound the proper but different claims on us of the past, the present and the future. The corresponding virtue would be one of knowing not only what the time is now, but how the past is best remembered or honoured in it and how the way we inhabit it will help shape the future. This is the virtue of 'time wisdom.'

7

Tragic Desires

That human beings are creatures that have desires as well as needs is almost too obvious a point to state; that the two overlap is also self-evident, and a mark of good health. We want the nutrition, exercise, shelter, companionship and stimulation that we need. But we may also want more than we need. Alternatively, our needs and our wants may be badly calibrated. We need a well-balanced diet, for example – maybe with lots of vegetable matter – and yet we fancy pie and chips. But it's not impossible to imagine – or indeed to know or to remember – that our desires can be morally disconnected. This is what happens when we want forbidden fruit of one kind or another. It is relatively straightforward when the forbidding has been done by an official or an authority outside ourselves. We struggle with it, but we still know where the line is drawn and that there will be consequences if we transgress. More complex and agonizing is the situation where we both want something and don't want to want it, or where the wanting of it is incompatible with our better, wiser and higher desires and aspirations.

These muddles are a consequence of freedom. Without free will it makes no sense to begin to discuss sin or vice in any form, and certainly not in the form of tragic desire. Without free will our wants and needs overlap completely; like two perfectly aligned circles in a Venn diagram, you can't see that there are actually two present. The experience of being human, however, is to know that your wants outstrip your needs.

Lust

Despite the fact that it is probably the best-known sin, the suggestion that lust is a part of the dark side of the soul could conceivably come across as strange and naïve in today's world; as if it had come from someone who had never seen a motion picture or browsed in a newsagent's shop. Far from being in the shadows, lust is in the limelight. As far as many are concerned, this is all very much for the best. Not only is it fun and pleasurable, it's also healthy. This much at least we learnt from Sigmund Freud. Lust isn't a problem unless it is unnaturally suppressed.

Although several churches and institutions have been scandalized by the revelation of the sexual abuse of children and vulnerable adults, it is in the institutions that try to keep lust in the dark, to deny or repress it, and that have fostered an ethos of secrecy, where the scale of the problem has been most severe. A major study on child sexual abuse in the Roman Catholic Church refuses the easy conclusion that the problem lies with the individual abusers – the few bad apples – and also eschews the idea that there are simple lines of causality between, for instance, sexual identity and abusive behaviour. Rather it concludes that the questions 'must be considered in the context of the overall context of the organization of the Catholic Church'. Discussing the issue of accountability the author writes that, 'rigidly hierarchical models of accountability that are accompanied by rigid hierarchies of power foster by their very nature mechanisms of denial and structural secrecy.' The point here is not that sex abuse claims were covered up, but that the secrecy, together with other factors, were intrinsic and significant aspects of the organization in which this happened. 'It is my contention', the author concludes, 'that children and young people were chosen for sexual and emotional expression by the participants in my research because they believed that all routes to adult sexual and emotional relationships were closed to them as part of the project of clerical life.' The key phrase for our purpose here is 'closed to them'. As we have seen, seeking to close off, or deny, the dark side of the soul doesn't work. Any account of the deadlies must take this into account both in its analysis and its prescriptions. When it comes to lust, like several other areas, it means being more realistic about the whole imperfect truth of people.

If the scandal of sexual abuse isn't sufficient to discredit the Church as a source of wisdom when it comes to matters of sexual energy, there is the extraordinarily corrosive sexism that has been rampant in the Church down the centuries. Evagrius, something of a hero in this tale so far, didn't have a good word to say about the female sex. For instance, it was Evagrius who wrote, 'The sight of a woman is a poisoned arrow; it wounds the soul and injects the poison, and for as long a time as it stays there it causes an ever greater festering.' We could move on to consider the way in which the Church has created a climate of exclusion, oppression and persecution of gay people.

No, the Church and its traditions are the last place many people today would be looking for wisdom about lust.

This sort of perspective is not uncommon, and is one of the factors that help form the cultural environment that sneers at the notion of sin, seeing it as a joke word, the easiest excuse for a laugh. But laughing is not simply a laughing matter. As Freud knew, jokes are never merely funny, they are also revelatory. Contemporary comedy is now almost completely naked in its allusion to sexual activities; so naked that the puzzle is no longer what is said or inferred but why people find it amusing. The comedy of sex depends on coyness, embarrassment, hidden-ness to make it work. If it's all out in the open what's there left to titillate our sense of humour? The end of this one might foresee as dull predictability and tawdry boredom, but something tells me that we are never going to be so liberated about our bodies, or about sex and sexuality, that there will ever be an end to smirking about sex, or the shock of finding that one is laughing with people about things that you would never talk with them about, but you now realize are part of your shared imagination – if not actual experience.

Just a few decades ago sexual comedy used to be very different. We had the endless 'Carry On' series and a string of male characters whose shameless lechery has become in retrospect a source of huge embarrassment. These middle-aged lechers got many of their laughs by parading their lust in public, revealing perhaps that they had never taken Evagrius to heart. It used to be standard family viewing, but middle-aged lechery isn't funny any more, or acceptable. It's just too creepy to see evidence of predatory lust that was not only unrequited but also unrequitable.

How are we supposed to read this? You could say that it was a typically patriarchal bloke thing, affirming men as subjects (even if rather creepy ones) and women as objects, in particular objects of salacious desire. On the other hand you could say this was a display of helpless vulnerability in the face of lust. Men putting themselves forward not as positive, heroic role models but as pathetic and sad figures of fun. The first reading is that we are invited to see the world through lecherous eyes, the second is that we are invited to laugh at those in the grip of lust. The first was funny-trangressive, and the second was funny-cruel. And perhaps it was either or both – depending. Comedy can indeed be complex and ambiguous. Either way, as we've observed, it's no longer funny. Yet the suggestion that this particular dark corner of our soul is now fully illuminated is not entirely convincing. Give it a few more years and today's stand-up comics will be seen through different eyes and a new generation of young people will wonder what on earth their parents were like to laugh at this stuff.

Sexual comedy has a long history. *Double entendres* have been nudging people into a knowing smile since at least the time of Chaucer. They depend on a complex dance of knowingness and naivety; they are puns that come to life because one of the meanings is 'naughty'. Lust may be normal and natural – after all, the species is going nowhere if people don't do the necessary to reproduce. This is both an evolutionary perspective and a biblical view – 'go forth and multiply', 'fill the earth and subdue it'. These are early and fundamental commandments to the human race according to Hebrew Scriptures, and Christianity has fully taken this on board. Lust may be normal and natural – but it's one thing to copulate for the future of the race, quite another to enjoy the process to such an extent that the means become much more important than the end.

The history of the notion that lust is sinful is as complex as any other history. There are elements of spirit–body dualism in there. There is misogyny in there too. There is worry and anxiety and embarrassment in there, and real frustration that the sexual imagination and the male sexual member seem to refuse to come under the control of the will or reason. And guilt, lots of guilt, and lots of shame. Which is precisely what you would expect if you try to control that which you know perfectly well is deeply resistant to control by making up rules and regulations for others to keep. It is interesting, though, that when they were placed in the Garden of Eden, the first couple were told not to touch the fruit of a certain tree. They were not told not to touch each other, nor not to look at each other, even in those pre-fig-leaf days. The interesting bit about the Garden of Eden, however, seems not to have been the sex but the forbidden. That at least is what brings the story to life. 'Who told thee that thou wast naked?' The point is that until they started breaking rules they had no idea, not that the first rules were in any way connected with the nakedness or with what came later to be covered.

The psychologist Simon Laham defines lust as 'activation of the sexual behavioural system' and describes some of the ways in which this activation or arousal influences people. Unsurprisingly, increased sexual arousal leads to people adopting behaviours that are likely to maximize their chances of sex. It also increases their tendency to focus on the present moment rather than the future and to perceive and think at the detailed local level rather than the big-picture, global level. Men are apparently inclined to take more risks when under the spell of lust. This is the 'lust-inspired risky shift', which occurs at both low and high levels of lust. One experiment involved asking skateboarders to do risky tricks when observed by either a male observer or an attractive female. As predicted, there were more risky tricks when the observer was an attractive female. This riskiness led to both more crash landings and more successfully completed tricks. There is also evidence that lust is related to creativity. This cuts two ways: people are more creative when aroused, and human beings seem to find creativity a desirable trait in a sexual partner.

Laham draws a line between the activation of the sexual behaviour system and sexual behaviour itself – seeing lust as the psychological state. In the Sermon on the Mount, Jesus blurs this boundary by saying, 'You have heard that it was said, "You shall not commit adultery." But I say to you that everyone who looks at a woman with lust has already committed adultery with her in his heart.' This sort of spiritualizing may be wise, but it can cause deep anxiety. Augustine agonized about the inability to find the on/off switch for sexual arousal, but neither agonizing nor making up rules seem to be the right way to deal with this reality. Recognizing that it is part of who we are, and creating a culture that seeks not to control but to manage the good and the corrosive aspects of this aspect of who we are, is a task that remains incomplete, however liberated we feel, and however much we laugh at, not with, our more immediate ancestors.

Harnessing lust to creativity and putting it in the context of values such as care and the common good are appropriate steps. It is interesting that when Mihaly Csikszentmihalyi writes about sex in *Flow* he focuses not on the short-term pleasures of anticipated and actual carnality, but on the effort needed to make sex an enjoyably bonding and fulfilling part of a long-term relationship. In fact he refers to three dimensions. These all have their own pleasures, but only the third has the capacity to make people happy and fulfilled in the long run. The first dimension is that of physical pleasure, which, he says, is easy, unskilled and potentially overwhelming – at least for a while. Then there is the romantic dimension, the cultivation of the skills of relating and sex – something he wryly comments is like sport in that many are inclined to let others make such efforts; for example, watching a romantic movie rather than behaving in romantic way. And the third dimension is the relationship of care. This is fed by mutual attentiveness (not, we might note, attraction; it's past that stage now) and leads on to an enjoyable and satisfying future by dint of the relationship becoming ever more complex and intricate.

There is no denying that Christianity has yet to get its relationship with lust, sexuality and the body into good order. The first two thousand years have been difficult in that regard. But the future is looking much brighter. The question, both for the individual and for the wider community, is whether lust can be drawn ever more fully into the service of care and love and the enrichment of life. The answer to this may depend on whether care and love and enrichment of life are serious top-level goals. If they are *not* then lust is doomed to being an embarrassing legacy of our animal inheritance and the source of humour that reflects the particular hang-ups created by changes in sexual mores from generation to generation. If they are, then lust can be seen as part of the process, one of the dimensions of deep relationships that depend on long-term commitment and the focusing of attention not on the attractiveness of possible future mates but on the needs, thoughts and feelings of the current partner. This, I venture, makes some sort of sense of Jesus' enigmatic remark. It boils down not to what you are staring or gawping at, but what you are most seriously paying attention to. Fulfilment comes not from following sexual arousal wherever it leads, but from the enrichment of a relationship that already has an erotic dimension. The vice of lust is that which pulls us away from the possibility of such fulfilment.

Greed

Although the word 'greed' has come to mean a variety of things in contemporary English, in the tradition of the deadlies it has its primary reference in the love of money. In his first letter to Timothy Paul writes that 'the love of money is the root of all kinds of evil' and Evagrius' third thought was focused on a Greek word that means 'love of silver' and has been translated as the word 'avarice'. Today this word means something like 'inordinate desire for gain – or wealth' and is part of a group of words that include the noun 'cupidity', and the adjective 'rapacious'. It is illuminating, however, to focus on the core idea of love of money.

It is sometimes noted by preachers that Jesus spoke much more about money than sex, whereas the contemporary church has it the other way around. Such commentators have not perhaps attended many local church meetings, where 'financial matters' are inevitably among the subjects that get a lot of attention, and meetings of the finance committee are frequent, lengthy and difficult. What the commentators have in mind is, rather, what the media choose to draw to the public's attention from the many deliberations of synods and councils and the numerous pronouncements of church leaders. The Church is, I suggest, just as caught up in matters of money as any other human community or organization today. It is unusual, though, in that, in theory at least, its concern about money is not about 'nicely calculated less or more' but about an aspect of the human heart in relation to money – seeing the *love of* money as deeply problematic.

Dante assigns the avaricious to the fourth circle of hell. They are not there alone. They share the space with the financially incontinent, the spendthrifts, the prodigals, with whom they are locked in endless and unwinnable conflict. This may indeed sound like a church finance committee meeting, but it is no joke for the established church if it examines more precisely what Dante imagines here, as he populates the avaricious side of this circle of hell with clergy, monks and popes. There is irony here, as the New Testament is so adamantly against personal wealth and in particular against seeking to purchase spiritual gifts with money. This goes back to the story of Simon the magician in the Acts of the Apostles and became known as the sin of simony. Financial dishonesty is also, in Acts, the cause of one of the most startling incidents in the whole Bible. This is the story of Ananias and Sapphira, a married couple who sold some property and, having said that they would donate all the money they made to the apostles, withheld some. When challenged, Ananias continued not to disclose the full extent of their financial gain and then, immediately afterwards, but quite independently, Sapphira did the same. Both dropped down dead within seconds of having reiterated their lie. Was it shame that killed them, or was it the hand of God? The Bible doesn't tell us. But we can read from this passage that there is disapproval of fraud, even in the context of a voluntary gift, at the very highest level.

Money is also at the very centre of two of the most famous sayings in the Bible. I am thinking of the occasion when Jesus is asked whether taxes should be paid, and he answers, having first got his religious challengers to tell him whose image they see on a coin, that they should 'render therefore unto Caesar the things which are Caesar's; and unto God the things that are God's'. Alongside this we might also rank Jesus' comment that, 'ye cannot serve God and mammon'. The message here is plain. God and money are in competition. They both seek our service and indeed our love. Or so it seems when we don't relate to money wisely.

Yet this does not mean that money is intrinsically bad. It just means that, like everything else, it isn't God. The point about money, however, is that people do sometimes relate to it *as if* it is God – that is, they can be fooled into 'loving' it. And it is by relating to money in this way that people fall into one of the vicious traps of sin. It is the trap of loving that which cannot return your love but will, over time, just suck you dry.

When people say that they 'love' a certain kind of food, or a way of spending their free time, what they mean is that they like it very much. There is no problem with this. It's just a figure of speech. But to love money is a serious mistake because it doesn't mean that they like it very much. Money, unlike certain foodstuffs, has no intrinsically likeable qualities. Although they may admire the design, no one says,

'I love twenty-pound notes.' This doesn't mean that people don't in some corrupt and corrupting sense 'love' money. Clearly they do. Relating to money with inappropriate desire, and giving it a priority and importance that is disproportionate, is precisely the vice that is in focus here. This is the image and the sadness of the avaricious – a mean-faced miser holding greedily on to his moneybags, while rapaciously wringing profit out of everything he can control. It's not that the avaricious make a lot of money – often they do not, as avarice doesn't necessarily make for good financial decision making. The point is that in an emotional and spiritual sense they make too much of it. Avarice is the sin of letting money be more than money in your heart. The avaricious are often imagined as clinging on to their money tightly. But avarice is not primarily a matter of behaviour. What looks like being 'tight' might just be a way of prudently making ends meet and taking a responsible longer-term view. Avarice is holding on to the cash with inappropriate feeling, as if the pile of money is a lover who promises to look after you in the years to come.

The seventeenth-century metaphysical poet Abraham Cowley says something like this – though in a rather different way – in his essay 'Of Avarice'.

There are two sorts of *Avarice*; the one is but of a Bastard kind, and that is, the rapacious Appetite of Gain; not for its own sake, but for the pleasure of refunding it immediately through all the Channels of Pride and Luxury. The other is the true kind, and properly so called; which is a restless and unsatiable desire of Riches, not for any farther end or use, but onely to hoard, and preserve, and perpetually encrease them. The Covetous Man, of the first kind, is like a greedy *Ostrich*, which devours any Metall, but 'tis with an intent to feed upon it, and in effect it makes a shift to digest and excern it. The second is like the foolish Chough, which loves to steal Money onely to hide it. The first does much harm to Mankind, and a little good too, to some few: The second does good to none; no, not to himself. The first can make no excuse to God, or Angels, or Rational Men for his actions: The second can give no Reason or colour, not to the Devil himself, for what he does; He is a slave to Mammon without wages. The first makes a shift to be beloved; I [ay], and envyed, too, by some People. The second is the universal Object of Hatred and Contempt.

And not only an object of hate and contempt – the avaricious miser is, no matter how wealthy, unhappy. As Benjamin Franklin is said to have put it, 'Avarice and happiness never saw each other.' Cowley proposes that while a person of virtue and wisdom may be content with little, an avaricious soul has nothing despite having everything. He renders this insight poetically.

> And, oh, What Mans condition can be worse
> Than his, whom Plenty starves, and Blessings curse;
> The Beggars but a common Fate deplore,
> The Rich poor Man's Emphatically Poor.

Without doubt the most famous contemporary passage on greed comes from the film *Wall Street* and is often paraphrased as a slogan of the 1980s, 'greed is good' – intended as an endorsement of the fetterless exploitation of free market economics as a kind of financial Darwinism – tough for some, but better for most in the long run. However, a closer look at the speech doesn't allow for quite such a straightforward designation of what is odious about the orator, Gordon Gekko.

> The point is, ladies and gentleman, that greed, for lack of a better word, is good. Greed is right, greed works. Greed clarifies, cuts through, and captures the essence of the evolutionary spirit. Greed, in all of its forms – greed for life, for money, for love, knowledge – has marked the upward surge of mankind.

Before either cheering the speech or deploring it, one might just ponder the phrase 'for lack of a better word'. It's as if the speaker knows that there is more than one kind of greed, and that he is struggling for lack of an adequately rich and nuanced vocabulary to talk about all this. Gekko is a repellent character, but that is not because of what he says in *this* speech, which is actually intended to motivate shareholders to challenge those who are freeloading from the company as unnecessary vice-presidents. If it is a pro-greed speech it is to rouse the many shareholders to rebel against the relatively few and excessively greedy company vice-presidents. Gekko is repellent not because he seeks to motivate the shareholders but because he is ruthless in his pursuit of success and is no stranger to corruption.

What I see here is not the relatively easy point about the transvaluation of values – rebranding the vice of greed as a virtue. A little greed, if it means an understanding of the value of money and the taking of financial responsibility, can be a good thing. Indeed, it is hard to argue, given the success of capitalism in improving the standard of living of the many, that the desire to make money and become reasonably well off is fundamentally problematic. The trouble is not when people make or make use of money but when they fall in love with it. Aristotle understood usury to be a bad thing, and Thomas Aquinas followed him on this point, because it was unnatural for money to breed. Jesus' and Paul's beef with money is similar but different. It's not that it can't breed but that, as the Beatles sang, it can't buy love or generate anything of spiritual value.

Exploring greed alone will not lead us to understand all the many spiritual, emotional and behavioural byways that are on the map of the relationship between human beings and money. It is however of significant interest to note that there is something wrong with us when we relate to that which is inert as if it were living and spiritual. This is the general problem of 'idolatry', of which 'love of money' is a particularly important example.

In Evagrius' 'love of silver' we can see echoes of the famous classical story of King Midas, who wished he could turn everything to gold, not realizing that rather than making for a rich life this would spread death. The story is apposite. It doesn't mean that money is a bad thing. It means that we can get our lives into a terrible mess, and also our communities and societies, when we relate to money as if it is something that it is not. Precious metal is of value because it is both inert and lustrous. This, however, makes it a means to an end, not a suitable object of love. So too the credit card and the bank balance.

One need not be seduced into the love of money, however, to be troubled by excessive accumulation, whether of money or things.

The strange inability of human beings to be satisfied is something that needs careful consideration at this particular point in the history of the human race. A little greed may be necessary to help move things forward socially and economically, but what might happen if greed were never to be satisfied, not only because neither money, nor material goods, nor purchased pleasures can return our affections, but because acquisition and consumption themselves become unstoppable and destructive habits? Insatiability is not on the traditional list of the deadlies – and it is different to both greed and gluttony, and yet it must surely be vicious for people to be discontented when they have their share of the good things of life.

Insatiability

How much is enough?' As well as being an excellent question, this is the title of a book by Robert Skidelsky and Edward Skidelsky – a father-and-son team who between them span the disciplines of economics and philosophy. Their book begins by puzzling over what they call 'Keynes's mistake'. It is indeed a good thing to ponder.

In 1930 John Maynard Keynes wrote an essay entitled 'Economic Possibilities for our Grandchildren'. In it he prophesied that as technology advanced so we would have to work less and less, and that humanity's most pressing problem would soon become 'how to use his [sic] freedom from economic cares'. Few prophets can have been more wrong – and so the question that the Skidelskys ask themselves is, 'What was it that Keynes failed to take into account?' Their answer is 'insatiability'. By insatiability they mean the inability to answer the question 'How much is enough?' Dropping briefly into the language of sin and vice, they speak of 'greed, envy and avarice' but they do not dwell for long on these words. But perhaps there is no need. The concept of insatiability points to something irrevocably restless that we view differently depending on whether we see it in others or ourselves. For instance,

I am diligent.

You are committed.

He or she is a workaholic.

Insatiability refers to the independence that desire has from satisfaction. It's an unsatisfied craving for more than one has. Of course there is an ironic possibility here – in that one might never be satisfied with any particular explanation of insatiability. This jolly suggestion is meant to imply that insatiability need not only be material. There are those who have seen the basis of insatiability in such individual restlessness, a lack of capacity for contentment in any area of life. You could say that Augustine was the first theologian of restlessness when, at the beginning of his *Confessions*, he wrote the lines that have so often been quoted and blended into prayers. Addressing God, he declares that 'our heart is restless until it rests in you'. Augustine's astonishingly influential theology of sin was not based on restlessness but on pride and lust. One might wonder how Western intellectual and social history might have evolved differently had Augustine theorized more about restlessness than about these other matters.

Getting back to the way we think about happiness and restlessness today, the idea that we find that we are happy not so much in the achievement of our desires but in the pursuit of their satisfaction – that we naturally enjoy our appetites – is common. This seems to be a muddled and inconsistent truth. Certainly there are pleasures of anticipation – the smells from the kitchen, gathering around the table, the first sip of wine, picking up the cutlery – but there are also pleasures of satiation – the courses completed, the bottles empty, the sitting back in a more relaxed way, the deeper unfolding of conversation, or the collapse into frivolity. Similarly with holidays and vacations – the anticipation and planning is all part of the pleasure, but so too is the trip home and the unpacking and settling back into a familiar routine when it is all over and as the memories begin to settle down. We might well wish, though, that it was all just about to start over again. And maybe that's part of insatiability – the endless capacity to find grounds for dissatisfaction.

Economists are interested in scarcity, and so suggest that what drives the insatiable me is the desire for something that I can see someone else has but that I lack. This comparative theory sounds a bit like an outworking of the traditional sin of covetousness or envy. I may have been to Dorset for a week but you went to Devon for a fortnight – suddenly my delight is tarnished by a tad of dissatisfaction. It's absurd, of course. Your being in Devon doesn't diminish in any way my pleasures in Dorset. But nonetheless it niggles; and such niggles have a habit of persisting, of developing a strident and resentful tone, and speaking to us not of how lucky we are but of how someone else is a bit luckier. Such dissatisfaction might be resolved by going to Devon for a fortnight the following year, or, imagine this, by tripping down to Cornwall for a month. But, oh no, who is the first person we bump into in Penzance, but someone who has just returned from six weeks in the Bahamas. Suddenly the envy of the person who had a fortnight in Devon has disappeared under a terrible thundercloud of new covetousness that threatens to spoil the Cornish holiday from the start.

Insatiability is apparently, and perhaps inevitably, a prevalent vice in the very rich. This is something that fundraisers have to think about. What is it that I can give the person who has more money than I can imagine in order to solicit from him or her a donation to the cause I am striving to fund? This is quite a conundrum, but is not actually as difficult as it would be if insatiability weren't a singularly persistent sin or vice. For one thing, if it were not, there would be no people around so rich that they could afford to make six- or seven-figure donations. Second, there is, in fact, a simple answer to the question 'what do people who are very rich want?' It's ironic, and it feels cruel even to mention it, but it is *not* things that are very expensive. Rather, what the very rich want are *things that money can't buy*.

This is something that should be on the curriculum of a training academy for professional fundraisers, as it makes raising money from 'major donors' relatively simple. You just have to find things that money can't buy, give them to rich people, and then work on their sense of specialness in such a way as to prompt them to enjoy another experience that money can't buy – the joy of giving away a huge amount of money to your cause. Come to me all ye very, very rich and I will give you an experience of largesse that will blow your mind. But such insatiable minds are only blown for a brief period. Sooner or later our delighted donor is going to come across something that will press their dissatisfaction button – maybe someone who has given more to an even worthier cause, or who was given an even more mind-blowing experience that money can't buy. So what our fundraising professional needs to do before the ink is dry on the cheque is to organize some especially desirable donor recognition. It has to have the quality of being something money can't buy, at the same time as being only available to those who have provided significant sums of money. This is the way the philanthropic world goes round. It's not run on virtue, but vice. Without sin it would stop – but so too would many of the problems for which we need to raise funds by soliciting donations – and so on, and so on.

I say this not to be miserable, but to keep playing on this theme of restlessness, which is so connected with insatiability. Some of the most important, humane and spiritual work we can do is to enter into vicious downward spirals and turn them into virtuous upward spirals. This is never easy, but it isn't always entirely impossible. It would, however, be a lot easier if at some late stage in the money-making-leading-to-philanthropic-giving process the demon of insatiability could be exorcized. That would remove the vexed problem of donor satisfaction, which donor recognition, as we have already suggested, is unlikely ever to achieve fully while insatiability rules.

I have drifted away from the Skidelskys' book, but clearly its ideas are very relevant to our project of understanding the web of sin and vice today. Several times they refer to the naivety of the views of social theorists and economists – pointing out that capitalist economics is doomed because it fails to recognize the need for some kind of moral constraint on the scope of desire, and because it too easily encourages what one might call 'the monetization of everything' –

the notion that you can reduce all values to monetary values and thereby compare everything on one scale. The wealth and status equation depends on this, yet in the end it fails, because even the uber-wealthy come to realize that they are not at the top of the value tree; they become conscious, due to a combination of active vices, vainglory, envy and avarice among them, not of macro-plenitude but of micro-lack.

The Skidelskys also talk about 'snob goods', and their discussion can throw a little light on this whole sorry business. Snob goods are things the value of which entirely depends on the fact that others do not have them because they cannot afford them. It's helpful to spell out the nasty side of this. These things derive their value from the admiration of those who see what it is that they don't have and only then come to desire it. This is doubly good news for the purveyors of snob goods. The first benefit is that as the value of that particular product increases in the eyes of those who don't have it so the market is able to produce and sell lesser simulacra. The second is that as soon as those who were deprived manage to acquire these lesser but nonetheless annoyingly convincing simulacra – the original snob is motivated to buy something that will recreate the distinction. This is the economic importance of the insatiable desire for status, the shadow side of which is that enough can never be enough. Or, as the Skidelskys put it, 'insatiability leads us away from the good life'.

Keynes's mistake was that he didn't understand or foresee the capacity of human beings to engage in want-creation that would always outstrip wealth-creation. Nor, it seems, did anyone else. Perhaps that was because they averted their gaze for too long from the dark side of the soul. The Skidelskys have an eye on it when they relate the joke of the oligarch who asks his friend how much his tie had cost. 'It was a thousand dollars.' 'Oh bad luck,' comes the reply. 'Mine was two thousand.'

Control

It's easy to know when we have come across a control freak, because we invariably find them annoying. We experience such characters as restricting us either by their insistence that we should do something by the book (of which they have a better understanding than we do) or by suggesting that they have personally devised a better way of going about things than we are employing. Control freaks are often prone to anxiety and unwittingly convey it as they seek to impose their will. They draw responsibility to themselves but push out anxiety. High-status control freaks tend to get away with all this, until they come across someone who is not inclined to be deferential. This is what happens in *Pride and Prejudice* when Lady Catherine de Bourgh, a singularly haughty control freak, is challenged by Elizabeth Bennet.

But control-freakery is not an endearing quality, and unless natural control freaks are very determined, it is unlikely that they will rise to the top. Rather they will exercise their irritating fastidiousness from the lesser domain of the administrator's position. Or at least that's where they should be, because a control freak who is under the control of a non-control freak is potentially very helpful. There is evidence, however, that those whom James Collins refers to as 'Level 4 leaders', those who are competent but *lack* the less egocentric

'Level 5' qualities of personal modesty and disinterested passion for the aims of the company or organization, are precisely those who are promoted to the most senior positions in organizations that have become anxious and uncertain.

If this were a book about managing people, the question would be how to make the best use of the control-freak qualities in your staff, while avoiding being pushed into reactive control-freakery by the anxiety that you experience as a result of your leadership responsibilities that seem to be greatly in excess of your actual authority and power. Control freaks often experience an authority deficit and this fuels their already significant anxiety and their desire to do something about it. In this way, control-freakery is one of the vices most prone to generating a vicious circle. However, this isn't a management book; it is an aid to introspection into the dark side of the soul. And so our question is not 'How do I handle the control freaks that surround me?' but 'Is there a control freak hidden in the shadows of my own inner being?'

And the answer to this question is 'Yes'.

The confidence of that answer comes from a remarkable book by psychiatrist Iain McGilchrist, called *The Master and His Emissary*, about the cultural implications of the divided human brain. To cut a very long story short, it's the left hemisphere that's the on-board control freak.

McGilchrist argues that the difference between the way the two hemispheres of the human brain operate is fundamentally connected with the forms of attention that are their norm. The right hemisphere is responsible for all forms of attention other than focused attention. It follows that the normal order of attending is for the right hemisphere to get a vague sense of what is going on and to determine what should be focused upon. That's step 1. Then the left hemisphere is set to work on detailed analysis. That's step 2. The results of this are passed back to the synthesizing and pattern-finding right hemisphere that, as the third step in the process, will add the information to the ever-developing big picture. This, at least, is what should happen. It is the process of wise perception.

Contrary to the traditional view that the left hemisphere is properly the dominant one, McGilchrist argues that it is the right that should predominate over the left. The right hemisphere is the 'master' of his title and the left hemisphere the 'emissary'. The title derives from a story where things get out of hand when a king is turned on by an emissary and killed. This, suggests McGilchrist, is the way it is between the hemispheres. The right, and properly dominant, hemisphere knows its need of the left, more analytic, hemisphere. However, the left hemisphere does not appreciate or 'understand' that its mode of perception and analysis is only helpful when placed in a larger, synoptic context. It therefore denies the need, necessity and existence of the right hemisphere's perceptions, and determinedly ignores and seeks to undermine them. McGilchrist adduces huge quantities of neuroscientific and cultural evidence to support his argument that the left hemisphere's way of working is gradually detaching itself from its proper context in the right hemisphere.

Given that it is the right hemisphere that gives us a sense of wholeness, of pattern, beauty, tolerance of ambiguity, irony, humour, empathy, a sense of the special significance of works of art and of human beings, this does not sound like very good news for the human race – all these things are under attack. It does, however, or so McGilchrist argues, sound very much like modernity. The left hemisphere loves breaking things down, analysing detail, abstracting and quantifying; it prizes objectivity, rationality and the like. But the point is not merely that the left hemisphere has a different, preferred and complementary way of operating, though at one level this is the point because, in an appropriate context – i.e., one framed by right-hemisphere activity – the left hemisphere has a vital and irreplaceable role to play in making human culture what it is at its absolute best. The left hemisphere also has its own value system and this is the inverse of the right hemisphere's. The right hemisphere's value system is reflected by Scheler's pyramid of values that has 'the holy' at the top supported by, at ever-lower levels, 'values of the intellect', 'values of vitality' and, at the lowest level, 'values of use and pleasure'. The left hemisphere simply inverts this – everything else is put at the service of use and pleasure (forgetting, of course, that use is a means to an end and that pleasures can be potentially problematic or hostile).

The similarity between the left hemisphere in your skull and the control freak at work is by now becoming all too apparent. We are all, in part, this way inclined, and we may well discover that we are very largely this way inclined if we suffer a stroke that wipes out our right hemisphere and leaves our left hemisphere to its own happy, but ultimately sad and lonely, devices. Should that ever happen we will discover that we become impatient with images and art and music, and that instructions, definitions and details become compelling. We will stop reading novels or watching movies and stare delightedly at spreadsheets and databases.

In the second half of his book, McGilchrist discusses the way in which this power struggle between the hemispheres has unfolded through history. Commenting on the ancient world he writes,

> once the left hemisphere started to believe that its dominion was everything, once the wealth it created began to remain obdurately in its own province, as though it could survive on its own, rather than being returned to the world that only the right hemisphere could bring about, then the empire – not the Roman Empire, which the world could do without, but the empire that the hemispheres between them had created, which we cannot – began to crumble.

The crumbling has taken a long time. The Renaissance was a good time for the right hemisphere but as it progressed toward the Enlightenment so left-hemisphere functioning began to predominate, with its focus on detail and its iconoclastic tendencies. At the Reformation, words prevailed, the pulpit triumphed over the altar, proclamation trumped sacramental manifestation and, to add a point of our own to the catalogue, the art of the seven deadly sins in visual poetic and narrative form was replaced by the Ten Commandments; not only a list of words, but a decontextualized and numbered list: heaven on earth for the left hemisphere.

What matters most of all about this is that while the right hemisphere knows that it needs the left, the left is in denial about its own need, and so construes its relationship with the right hemisphere as competitive and antagonistic. The left hemisphere is interested in power, control and domination. This is the tragic aspect of focused, precise and analytic attention that has lost its context and humility, together with its sense of relatedness, relationality or interdependence.

But it's the cognitive correlate of control-freakery that is particularly interesting in McGilchrist's understanding of the left hemisphere and its will to power. He writes that,

> The power-hungry will always aim to substitute explicit for intuitive understanding. Intuitive understanding is not under control, and therefore cannot be trusted by those who wish to manipulate and dominate the way we think; for them it is vital that such contexts, with their hidden powerful meanings that have accrued through sometimes millennia of experience, are eradicated.

At the end of his book he declares that even if this story about the cerebral hemispheres proves to be 'just a metaphor' he will be content. And so, perhaps, should we. For the argument has connected the desire to control with a certain cognitive style that is alive and well in the control freak and which, if we are honest in our introspection, is part of the way we operate. There is a time and a place for focused attention and analytic, abstract thinking and the actions that derive rationally from it. But the virtue of this cognitive package quickly degenerates not only into a vice but into a fractious vicious circle if it manages to wriggle from the context that it believes to constrain it with irrelevancies, but which is, in fact, the *sine qua non* of its value.

Control, in other words, deserves its place. It is a natural and necessary desire, but tragic when it predominates.

8

Malicious Tendencies

I once had occasion to be extensively involved in the aftermath of the murder of a teenage boy. As the months of a deeply dispiriting year went by, and the horror of the boy's suffering began to emerge from forensic evidence, the most chilling aspect of the situation was that the crime seemed to be without motive. Killed by a gang high on alcohol and other drugs, the 'why' question was answered by a shrug of the shoulders. Nobody knew. Nobody had a good explanation. It wasn't revenge. His torture started because the gang found him irritating. His protestations and cries of pain perhaps had a similar effect, and someone then decided that he should be shut up for good. And then disposed of in bin-bags around the town. 'Irritating' didn't work as an explanation, however, even if the irritated were high on drink and drugs.

It was troubling not to have an explanation, or to believe that the hints of cause added up to anything that might answer the why question. For some time I felt that to say that people did this simply because they found, in their intoxicated state, that they *could* do it, was helpful. Now I am no longer satisfied with this line of thinking. Rather I return to the awful thought that there is, somewhere in the dark side of the soul, a completely lightless and airless corner that sometimes unaccountably generates spite, malice and cruelty – the desire to hurt and harm. The only difference that 'power' makes is the extent and kind of harm that is done. Such malicious tendencies are manifest in toxic or vicious rage, as well as in a desire we tend to accept as an inevitable part of life – the desire for revenge. This is not going to be pleasant reading, but we do have to go to this dark corner. Let's begin with cruelty.

Cruelty

Is cruelty a sin? Is it vicious to be cruel? These questions have a strange ring to them. Cruelty is repellent and abhorrent. It disgusts us when we see it or hear of it, and it frightens us when we think that we might be on the receiving end of it. Torture comes to mind. We are in someone else's power. There is no escape. There are no windows. The walls are so thick, we are told, that no one will hear our screams. Our only company is a gang of people whose primary expertise is in the infliction of pain. We know that they will be good at their job and we can see in their eyes and demeanour an enthusiasm for the task. The only thing holding them back is their knowledge that we are already in acute suffering as we anticipate what might be in store for us. We know that what will happen, and how it will make us feel, is beyond our imagination. We also know that all too soon this fear of the unknown will be replaced by excruciation that will make our own death our only desire.

This is what cruelty does. Is it a sin? It's not listed among the seven deadlies, and there is no mention of it in the Ten

Commandments. Evagrius, as we know, was more troubled by the noonday demon than by thoughts of hurting or being hurt. Augustine was troubled by lust and its persistent resistance to control and the dividedness and weakness of will that it signalled, and Aquinas saw all sin as flowing from the corruption of spiritual pride. This is not to say that there is no cruelty in the Bible or in religious iconography. Very many horrible things happen in the Old Testament. In the New, cruelty is inflicted on the faithful but not reciprocated.

To be cruel is to intend and cause others to suffer. Judith Shklar says that the suffering must be physical and the intention must be to cause anguish and fear. Cruelty is the wilful inflicting of suffering on another person. This can only be done when there is a power differential, but we still entertain cruel thoughts and fantasies about those who are our peers or our superiors – wishing them ill for whatever reason. Maybe out of envy, but maybe – well maybe just because we wish them ill, because of a malicious tendency within us of which we are largely unaware. *Schadenfreude*, pleasure in another's misfortune, is connected with cruelty. It is similar but different to vicious envy – which is displeasure at another's good fortune. We might wonder whether *schadenfreude* is itself a vice or sin. It certainly fits with the Evagrian idea of 'hostile pleasure'. Not a feeling to be proud of, despite the fact that we catch ourselves enjoying it when he or she does at last get his or her comeuppance.

Cruelty and *schadenfreude* meet when we contemplate medieval depictions of hell. Different feelings blend when we behold the earlier iconography of persecution and martyrdom, or when the cross of Christ is surveyed. Theology tells us to read love and sacrifice, glory and triumph from that cross. But the most immediate message is of physical pain and suffering, together with loneliness and abandonment. It is an astonishing image to put in front of children and anyone capable of empathy. If it had not come to us down the centuries we liberal and sensitive moderns would be disgusted, outraged and appalled, and in a fit of superiority would ban the image not on religious grounds but on the basis of good taste and decency. And on ethical grounds too. One wouldn't want to put ideas into anyone's mind. Certainly the theology is that this was a once-and-for-all sacrifice that takes away the sins of the world, and it is not part of the gospel, in which the story of the cross is ultimately transcended, to suggest that anything like this needs to be emulated or repeated. But that's very much in the small print. The stronger message, the spirituality of contemplating crucifixion, in these days when most physical cruelty is kept out of the public gaze, involves some kind of unconscious accommodation to the horror of excruciating suffering.

Shklar credits Montaigne with putting forward the first spirited attack on cruelty. In doing so he was announcing a particular vice – one that was neither religious nor political. 'It [cruelty] is a vice that disfigures human character, not a transgression of a divine or human rule.' By putting cruelty at the head of his list of ordinary vices, Montaigne was reacting against Machiavelli, who had argued that political leadership involved the ruthless use of power to instil fear in the governed. 'It is far safer to be feared than to be loved' is the most famous saying from his political treatise *The Prince*. But Montaigne was also whistle blowing against a Christianity that not only condoned but inflicted and perpetuated cruelty, not least where it was most zealous – Montaigne's eye was on the behaviour of the Christians in the New World.

We might also consider putting violence alongside cruelty, but cruelty need not be physical or involve bodily pain. Then again, violence is not necessarily physical either. Some language is violent. At the core of violence is the idea of *violating* another person, and that implies something active and invasive, whether physical, mental or spiritual. Cruelty need not be violent or violating; it can involve intentional withdrawal and active avoidance. It can also take the form of malicious gossip or intriguing against someone in such a way that they become isolated or lose important sustaining relationships.

Is cruelty based on hatred? Do you have to hate someone to be cruel to them? The answer here is probably not. Cruelty could spring from other sources: a desire to be noticed by someone who is ignoring you, for instance, or an attempt to impress a third party. The torturer need not hate the torture victim. He or she may merely be afraid of being tortured him or herself.

The question of whether punishment is cruel is a tricky one, and views change all the time. Today the thought of someone being broken on a wheel or hung, drawn and quartered will be immediately understood as cruel, but such punishments were accepted as appropriate in Montaigne's time. We have already noticed that corporal punishment in school has long since had its day, but one might wonder whether a physical punishment, quickly and dispassionately delivered, is necessarily more cruel than punishments that humiliate, embarrass or deride an individual. Is it cruel to imprison people knowing that they are likely to be socialized into the ways of crime, become increasingly dependent and institutionalized, and very likely to suffer boredom? Beating people is barbaric, but boring them for extended periods is acceptable. They may, however, both be equally cruel.

We are, it seems, in a strange cultural place regarding cruelty. We hate and abhor it in its physical and violent forms, but are not as sensitive to its more subtle and insidious manifestations. But our concern here is less with cultural expression than with understanding the dark and dangerous aspects of ourselves. Can we admit to having a shard of cruelty in our own soul? It would, I suggest, be wise to do so, even if we intend to excise it, like a nasty splinter in our thumb.

And if we confess to cruelty, can we also admit to spite? In a recent book, *Seven Deadly Sins*, Aviad Kleinberg recalls the time when he secretly destroyed the miniature city that a fellow pupil at his school, Micky, had built in the sand. The context here was that Micky, a shy, friendless and artistic boy who was much bullied and often had his constructions destroyed when he made them in the school grounds, had gone out to the surrounding wastelands to create in a place that others would not see. This is relevant because, as Kleinberg emphasizes, there was no social advantage to be gained by his act of vandalism. Kleinberg reflects on his actions as follows.

I remember studying that magnificent construction for a while, and then destroying it. I knocked down everything – roads, bridges, trees. I don't think I enjoyed the destruction. I'm quite sure I was immediately invaded by a strong feeling of shame. I understood that I had become just like the barbarians, the classmates I both detested and envied . . .

I cannot pretend to have surrendered to social pressure. The act of destruction was not a means of gaining acceptance by a gang . . . In school I did not belong to any group. Indeed, not-belonging was my main attribute. Besides, nobody knew I had destroyed the little city – not even Micky – and I find it hard to believe that my feat of senseless vandalism would have impressed boys. This was solitary trespassing.

Kleinberg goes on to describe how he resonated with Augustine's account of stealing pears when he was young. For Augustine, the pleasure was not in the pears but in 'doing what was not allowed'. And, in Kleinberg's translation of Augustine, 'I had no motive for wickedness except wickedness itself. It was foul and I loved it . . . I was seeking not to gain anything by shameful means, but shame for its own sake.'

Cruelty, spite and malice are real vices. We make spiritual and human progress not by denying that they are any part of us but by recognizing that, inexplicable as they may be, they probably are.

Rage

Before examining the vice of rage, or as it is often put, wrath, there are several questions that clamour for attention. The first is 'Why is it in the list at all?' For one thing it is natural and proper to be angry when things are wrong. When you see cruelty or injustice, for instance, it is right and good that anger flares up. It is an important motive, and to give it a bad name is itself a serious error. Surely we should be rehabilitating anger, not besmirching it as a sin?

This question can be easily answered.

As I write this chapter the national and local papers are reporting the tragic death of a much-loved seventy-nine-year-old man, Mr Don Lock. Mr Lock received multiple stab wounds after he was attacked by the driver of another motor vehicle with whom he had what the papers are calling a 'minor prang'. The tragedy is being described as 'road rage' and has all the ingredients one might expect. The pretext for the attack is not based on any prior relationship between assailant and victim. The context – a pleasant rural village in West Sussex on the A24 – is benign. As someone commented on the regional news report, 'nothing ever happens round here'. The only thing we know is that the assailant had a big knife in his car and that the car was a 'classic'. When interviewed by journalists after the event, neighbours of the assailant described him as 'meek, mild mannered and subdued' and 'not the aggressive type'.

It is a terribly sad story, and what people say about the character of Don Lock himself, a cancer survivor who cycled 150 miles a week, loved his six grandchildren and wife of fifty-five years, makes it all the more tragic. Looking for an explanation and a suitable expression of disdain, one of his grandchildren described the attacker as 'sick'. No one has suggested thinking of such 'murderous rage' as a sin or a vice. As we have seen, the vocabulary is not considered to carry sufficient weight in our culture today. However, if the incident has been accurately reported then it seems to be an account of what happens when the passion of anger is not a good reaction to injustice but a destructive expression of a vice.

A second question is also important, however, at least for the religious believer. 'Is not anger something which, while sometimes "sick", is more generally seen as a good thing, at least in religious tradition and teaching?' For do we not see in some of the greatest of spiritual guides and gurus some native and raw anger? Moses was furious when he came down the mountain to find the Israelites worshipping a golden calf. He threw the two tablets of the law to the ground and smashed them in his rage. Elsewhere in the Old Testament there are very many occasions when God was angered. In the traditional translation of the book of Psalms, the magnificent Psalm 78 has the most dramatic depiction not only of the ten plagues inflicted on the Egyptians, but also of God's response to wrongdoing. 'When the Lord saw this he was wroth . . . He smote his enemies in the hinder parts.' And lest we think it is only the Old Testament God who could be angry, there is more than a case of 'like Father like Son' in the New. The most famous episode is when Jesus overturned the tables in the Temple, but there are plenty of other occasions when he used his tongue to lash those he thought were oppressing the poor or exploiting position or piety to the wrong ends. And moving on to Paul there is clear evidence not only of a quick temper, but also of the kind of anger that gets into print. Parts of the epistle to the Galatians read like the sort of email someone sends you at 11.30 at night when they are really annoyed.

Taken together, these two questions force us to realize that when it comes to anger or wrath, or ire or indignation, we are not dealing with one simple human emotion or character trait but something more subtle and complex. Indeed, we are dealing with something – anger – that in itself is not good or bad, but that can be on some occasions excellent but on other occasions positively evil. Admittedly, it seems unlikely that were this book about virtues there would be a chapter on anger, but that is perhaps a mistake of the imagination all too typically made by writers of books about virtues. There is a place for good anger and righteous indignation, and believing that to be true does not remove the truth that anger can also be a vice; one that hurts both those who are on the receiving end, and those who are on the giving end. Vicious anger is always a kind of inner disturbance that takes root and grows because we indulge it in some way. The anger that is a vice is the indulgence of an aspect of our inner life that disturbs us deeply. This is the troubling 'thought' or 'passion' of anger that mattered very considerably to the hermit Evagrius: 'Anger is a passion that leads to madness and easily drives those who possess it out of their senses; it makes the soul wild and moves it to shun all (human) encounter.' And one certainly gets the sense that Evagrius himself had a bit of a temper: 'Anger is a passion that rises very quickly', he writes, presumably on the basis of his own eremitic experience.

> Indeed, it is referred to as a boiling over of the irascible part and a movement directed against one who has done injury or is thought to have done so. It renders the soul furious all day long, but especially during prayers it seizes the mind and represents to it the face of the one who hurt it.

Wrath involves a misuse of imagination, impression or understanding of others. It is not only vicious but malicious.

In contemporary idiomatic English there are very many phases that are commonly used to describe the process of becoming angry – 'I saw red', 'my blood boiled', 'I was spitting feathers', 'he went ape' (or bananas), 'she spat out her dummy' and/or 'threw all her toys out of the pram' and so on. On one occasion when I was leading a workshop on forgiveness I asked people to come up with a list of as many such expressions of anger as possible. The exercise went on much longer than I had planned and two things about it genuinely surprised me. The first was that the list was very long; it went on for several sheets of flip-chart paper. The second was how very much people *enjoyed* the exercise. They seemed to delight in the phrases themselves. They liked remembering them, saying them out loud, and as time went by so they grew bolder in egging each other on to remember and share more. But as well as the social thrill (these people had never shared quite like this before) there was, it seemed to me, a happy appreciation of the verbal imagination and wit that had at some point been exercised in coining these various phrases. Moreover, I suspected at the time, and I haven't changed my view on this, that the exercise itself rekindled for the participants something of the intrinsic pleasure of irritation. Indeed, so pleasurably cathartic was this exercise that I considered incorporating a blank page into this book right here to give the reader space to list all the 'I am angry' phases they can recall. I haven't done so . . . but there is always the inside back-cover.

The point I am making here is that there is something paradoxical about that part of the dark side of the soul that nourishes and breeds wrath. You could think of it as a nursery where grievances and grudges are looked after, encouraged and nourished until they come to maturity. In this regard I am suggesting that wrath has a very similar structure to lust – except that in lust we are *attracted to* our fantasy of another, whereas in wrath we are *repelled by* our inner fantasy of another. Both – like snobbery, envy and hatred – are sins of relating, or sins against mutuality, and like all these, and unlike cruelty, they subsist not in the darkest corners of our dark side but in the relatively well-illuminated bits. We know what's going on here; we palpably and knowingly enjoy it! What we don't appreciate is that these ways of relating to others through our fantasies of them are, in fact, isolating us and helping to create a social environment in which 'they' are robbed of some of their dignity and as a result end up losing out in subtle ways.

The vice of wrath, therefore, has nothing to do with the anger which is a response to injustice, or the righteous indignation that we appropriately feel when we see the weak and vulnerable put to further suffering at the hands of the powerful or cruel. We might well question whether our own fantasies of revenge, and our geeing up of our wrathful feelings about real or imagined slights, are actually connected with the horrors of murderous road rage, and in truth it is hard to make absolutely convincing causal connections. It certainly seems to be the case that at least some incidents of explosive and catastrophic rage come from mild-mannered and meek people who are not forever blowing off steam and frustration and breathing threats. But who is to say what was really going on in the minds and hearts of these apparently blameless individuals? The strangest thing to me about the sad story of the road rage that led to the death of Don Lock was that his assailant had stowed in his classic car a knife that could be used to stab someone to death, and that he thought to grab it as he went to the fatal altercation on the central reservation on the A24. There was something behind this, and while we can see why some might call it 'sick' it might be wiser to think of that word referring more to the nausea we feel when we picture the scene than as being a serious suggestion about causality.

Yet we do say that people who do unimaginable things are 'sick' – or 'mad'. As Mary Midgely explains with characteristic candour, it is when faced with malicious actions that our lazy everyday determinism that assumes a cause for everything outside ourselves lets us down.

> When we ask why things go as badly as they do in the world, and when we have finished listing the external, physical causes, most of us will have been struck by a thumping residue of human conduct which seems quite unnecessarily bad. We often call this conduct 'mad'. By this we commonly do not mean to give a definite medical diagnosis, pointing to actual mania or brain-damage resulting from lead-poisoning. We mean rather just to throw up our hands, to declare that we don't understand it.

To call wrath a sin, and to see it as the way in which we use others as fantasy figures whose faults allow us to feel good about our own hostility and negativity, is not a causal explanation for any particular event. But to say that it is not an important part of the story of who we are and how we relate to others, and that it does not contribute in subtle ways to our character, our relationships our society and ultimately the common good, is to deny the importance of this part of the dark side of the soul.

Revenge

But what of revenge? Whereas rage flares up wildly and delivers vicious satisfaction when indulged, is revenge a more measured response to something bad that has happened? No, that's not the difference. Revenge can be as quick as rage, and part of it. As Trudy Govier has put it, 'when we seek revenge, *we seek satisfaction by attempting to harm the other (or associated persons) as a retaliatory measure*'. And, despite what people have sometimes said, you can't get your retaliation in first. Retaliation is always a response, but it is not always a calculated or cool one.

And yet revenge isn't a necessary consequence of having been harmed. There are other ways of reacting when hurt has been felt deeply. For instance, believing perhaps that it was deserved (as the abject might), or just putting up with it (an 'acedic' response), or making an appropriate protest or legal complaint against the assailant, or both complaining and seeking some kind of peaceful equilibrium in and through forgiveness. There are many other possibilities too, and so whatever else revenge is, it is not fully determined by the actions of another or others. Despite what people may protest should their revenge get them into trouble, there were indeed other choices and courses of action available.

None of which means that revenge is necessarily wrong, but it is as well to admit that it is generally frowned upon in polite society. Hitting back, biting back, getting one's own back – these are familiar enough both in word and deed, but they are all seen as ways of taking the law into one's own hands. There may be reasons to do this, at least in the mind of the vengeful. The actual responsible authority may be seen as incapable of properly appreciating the gravity of the offence, or of dealing with it appropriately; the avenger may feel that someone needs to be taught a lesson 'that they won't forget' – and doubt whether the authorities can be trusted to mete out anything sufficiently memorable. Such, we might imagine, are the stories that the vengeful tell themselves.

Govier acknowledges all this, but also explores the question we raised under the heading of rage: that there may be an element of enjoyment here. 'Underlying the moral case for revenge is the assumption that *it can sometimes be right for a person to be the agent of deliberately bringing harm to another person, for the sake of enjoying having brought that harm.*' Although clearly disquieted by this underlying assumption of the place of personal enjoyment in the achievement of satisfaction that adds up to the justice achieved by revenge, Govier considers three reasons why that enjoyment might be justified. First, that the desire for revenge is 'natural'; second, that this is after all the foundation of our sense of justice; and third, that it lies at the core of the notion of retributive justice. What these various arguments all seek to do is to rehabilitate what we might call the vengeful urge. Whether or not this urge should be thus rehabilitated, it is not quite the same question as whether or not revenge is justified. For it might be that the vengeful urge is itself a vice or a sin – something that is part of who we are, and which needs to be accommodated in our character in ways that are not destructive to ourselves or to others. To put this in more overtly religious terms: this urge might be better understood as a temptation.

Put like this, the revenge question is not so very difficult. There is no need to deny the truth that, when we have been hurt, or when we have seen others hurt, we crave the satisfaction of some kind of proportional comeuppance for the perpetrator. Gilbert and Sullivan's *Mikado* desires to let the punishment fit the crime, and on a more epic and serious scale, this is the way in which Dante organizes both hell and purgatory. This can be read as a subtle commentary on the way in which vices backfire on those overcome by them, but there are other readings too – some more like the Hindu notion of karma, and some that are crude projections of the vengeful urge into the afterlife and onto the divine or the devil – depending on who you imagine to organize the punishment regime of hell and the purging and reforming processes of purgatory. We visited this less than flattering but nonetheless human reality when we briefly considered *schadenfreude*, but revenge is different. Revenge is when we precisely do not trust it to fate or time or the deity or the authority structures of the judiciary to turn the tables, but set about it, whether with a furious temper or with wilful glee, ourselves.

Another justification of revenge might be found in the notion that the suffering of the offender vindicates the victim, and it is this vindication that is the source of satisfaction, rather than a less savoury pleasure at the suffering of the offender. It will not be argued here that the desire for vindication takes the form of a vice or a sin, and yet nor is it a legitimate basis for revenge as understood here – inflicting suffering on another in the pursuit of satisfaction. Other methods of vindication are available that do not involve indulging the vengeful urge, such as giving an account of what has happened. That there is no one who will pay attention to this account, or that the victim is effectively voiceless, does not justify revenge either. It does, however, identify the need for protest or symbolic action to precipitate the social change that will allow the victim to be heard. This might in fact be an important tactic in the interests of justice, especially where there has been complicity, negligence or cover-up of crimes or other hurtful behaviour. It's expecting a lot of a victim of a harmful experience or shattering set of experiences to engage in protest rather than revenge; but it is the right thing to ask and to encourage. Revenge is too dangerous a strategy to embark on, both for the sake of the vengeful individual and for the community or society in which they are located.

The reason for this is to do with the impossibility of revenge ever working out in the way that its apologists and protagonists might hope. It is simple to see that this is so (at least it is easy when one is feeling dispassionate, and not in the grip of the vengeful urge prompted by yet more unreasonable or harmful behaviour by an especially annoying adversary). The logic goes like this: revenge is unlikely to be the end of the matter unless (a) victim and aggressor agree on their analysis of the event that provoked the victim to act on their vengeful urge, and (b) they also agree on the appropriateness, proportionality and validity of the act of revenge. In short, for the ethics of vengeful 'tit for tat' to work, all have to agree that 'tit' was wrong and needs to be redressed, and that 'tat' has achieved this in a way that the avenged feels is satisfying and the avenged-against accepts as satisfactory. Acceptable at a very low level of physicality in the playground and on the sports field – that is, when playing – or in verbal repartee – another form of play, 'tit for tat' is a dangerous process that inevitably tends towards escalation, not because anyone intends escalation when they embark on it, but because of the way in which the same events are viewed by different people.

9

The Web of Sin

The traditional seven deadly sins dominated the Christian imagination in the Middle Ages. The Enlightenment, Renaissance and Reformation, however, created a climate that was not congenial to thinking in terms of that rather incoherent list and it was replaced by the Ten Commandments. Since then there have been extraordinary and positive developments in ethical and psychological thinking. We look at ourselves and our world very differently to our medieval ancestors, partly because we know a lot more and partly because we face rather different issues. There are other reasons too, all of which add up to suggest that a static and disjointed set of seven deadlies is unlikely to be of help to us today in understanding ourselves or navigating our social and civic relationships, or even our relationship to God, should we believe in God – something that was axiomatic when the seven deadly sins had their heyday.

Or so might run an argument for leaving the seven deadly sins where they are – in the art, piety and theology of the past. Except for one thing. Although there was definitely a period in which the seven deadly sins were a static list, there was also an era of dynamism and change in the way in which they were understood and in terms of what was on the list. Moreover, as we have seen, when Evagrius the hermit put together the list of passions, thoughts or demons that set in place the foundation stone of this aspect of our spiritual history, he was not thinking of things to be guilty about or to be punished for, but of movements of mind, heart or soul to be wary of because they were hostile pleasures, and potentially problematic passions. Over the decades and centuries the passions became sins, and the responsibility for dealing with them moved from internal monitoring and self-regulation to the external and objective domain. We don't need to impugn the motives of the leaders who became the architects of these developments to recognize that the shift from understanding and dealing with inner passion and actual temptation personally, to understanding it instead forensically as sin – to be controlled by organization, law and imposed penance – was a fundamental paradigm shift. When at the Reformation the deadly sins with all their messy realism were replaced by the juridical commandments, and when to this was added Victorian concern about sexuality that reinforced the legacy of Augustine in this area, it became inevitable that as soon as religious institutions began to lose their power the notion of sin would be discredited. Indeed, undermining the notion that 'sin' might be a meaningful word has been one of the more subtle projects of secular modernity.

That task has now been almost fully achieved. The word 'sin' doesn't seem either sensible or useful today. As writers as different as Francis Spufford and the theologian Alistair McFadyen have pointed out, the word 'sin' has come to mean something very different in everyday talk today. Now it is a word to evoke not shame or concern, but a smirk or a titter. Sins are not seen as hostile pleasures, but as trivially naughty ones. When, on the other hand, we are appalled by the motives or actions of others we find that the word 'evil' comes to our lips, suspecting that what we observe and abhor is generated not by the likes of you and me but by someone who is very different, deep down. And when we are seriously concerned about someone's unhappy capacity to trouble him or herself, we don't ask whether this is the product of sin or vice, but whether there is a mental health issue that can be addressed.

Sin-talk is dismissed not because the sort of insight that Evagrius articulated is repudiated on its own terms – as part of the everyday art of self-understanding and demon wrestling. Rather it is because that tradition was corrupted over the years and seen in the end to represent just another control mechanism set up by a self-interested and hypocritical oligarchy. My aim here is not to seek to reintroduce the deadlies as a means of discipline and control, but as aids to self-understanding and to responsibility-taking in today's world.

Sin Suits its Times

To help do this we might put this story of the deadly sins in the context of an even longer historical sweep, and turn to the work of scholars such as Paula Fredriksen, who has made a detailed study of sin in the first five hundred years of the Christian era. In her conclusion she asserts that 'ancient ideas of sin ... are, like all human products, culturally constructed ... At the end of the day, howsoever defined, "sin" suits its times.' She certainly manages to show a wide variety of understandings of sin in her study of Jesus, and Paul, various Gnostics and then Origen and Augustine.

At the end of her study, Fredriksen turns her mind to the question of sin today. Recognizing that the word is not much used in everyday exchanges, she reflects on how people talk about their wrongdoing and reports, 'I am struck by the ways that ostensible acknowledgements of culpability minimize or even efface personal agency, thus responsibility.' For Fredriksen, sin has simply become 'error'. She suggests that people do not say that they are culpable, but that they have made a blunder. As she observes, responsible figures who have done wrong and been caught out often adopt the passive voice. 'Mistakes were made', they say. If they are bolder they might say, 'I made a mistake', but we rarely hear anyone say, 'I did something wrong.' What we have lost, she believes, is a sense of personal responsibility.

Might thinking about sin, not in the sense of sin as transgression of a law, but as a deep, hidden, important and yet potentially destructive aspect of who we are, help us to reclaim a positive sense of personal responsibility?

The argument of this book is that it is possible to answer this question positively, and for this reason it has explored the possibility of rekindling the tradition of deadly sins and vices, suggesting that these aspects of our soul are so dynamic and murky that they cannot be pinned down in once-and-for-all ways, but are best approached in everyday language and with the resources of art and culture and personal introspection. As part of this project it is necessary also to rehabilitate the notion of 'original sin'. A modern sense of original sin isn't intended to *explain* anything, but is needed to create the personal and spiritual space that allows us both to recognize that we can't quite account for ourselves, and at the same time to take responsibility for the whole of ourselves. Similarly, a sense of original sin is an important democratizing and levelling doctrine. Contrary to popular views today, to believe in original sin is not to have vicious self-regard, but to help move yourself away from the position where you regard either yourself or others viciously, whether that takes the form of snobbery, vanity, envy, arrogance, conceit or abjectness, or whether it issues in malicious behaviours like cruelty, rage or revenge.

To a post-Enlightenment rationalist Fredriksen's conclusion that '"sin" suits its times' might sound offensively relativistic, but it fits precisely with the picture that has been emerging in this exploration of the dark side of the soul. And the picture is this: that there is helpful wisdom in the tradition that we have summarized as the deadlies, but it is not the wisdom of believing that the numbered list is a complete and comprehensive description of everything that is rotten in the soul of a human being. Rather, it is the wisdom of pointing to some of the areas of life where we self-deceive, or overreach ourselves, or are seduced not by objects out there so much as by the insatiable nature of our desires, the viciousness of the way we look at others as well as ourselves, our confusions about time and money, and our desperation to take control.

Among the arguments of this book, the following are worth underlining at this point. First, the inherited list of deadly sins or vices is too short for practical and personal purposes. And second, that while some sins and vices are more manifestly or extremely toxic than others, this is not in itself an overridingly important consideration. Far more important is the complexity and subtlety of the web of sins that is woven by, around and within each personality and each culture.

The ancient tradition was increasingly dominated by the idea that pride was the root and source of all sin. This is not what Evagrius taught, but pride came to the fore in Gregory's understanding, influenced as he was by Augustine. It is this sort of thinking that generates the character of Satan, the angel who not only slipped but fell from the highest zenith of heaven, the company and presence of God, to the lowest and most distant depths of hell because he couldn't tolerate not being 'number one'. It is clearly a powerful myth, and has a frighteningly salutary ring to it when we consider those who have fallen from grace not because they are thoroughly rotten but because one great and foolish sin has undone them.

As Mary Midgely puts it,

> What brings Satan down is pride, the inability to tolerate anyone above him. This fault stands out all the more clearly because he still has all his native power and intelligence, and also a whole range of virtues – courage, resolution, enterprise, loyalty, even compunction and self-sacrifice in his willingness to volunteer for the dangerous mission to earth.

This is indeed tragic. We are fascinated and appalled by the pathos of there being one grating dissonance within an otherwise admirable character; a glaring fracture in the integrity of our hero. More common by far are we lesser mortals; moral minnows who are not undone by one huge metaphysical and damning gamble, but are wrapped up in a thousand micro-vices and petty sins: filaments so thin that they are invisible to the naked eye. Sometimes, like Satan in *Paradise Lost*, we are undone – or bound fast (choose your metaphor of preference) by one major sin. However our everyday experience is often less dramatic and, like Gulliver in Lilliput, we are captured by a multitude of tiny filaments, none of which on their own seem at all significant. Indeed they are, in most lights, quite invisible. This is the paradigm that I suggest works best for most of us most of the time: the web of sin.

A third point is pertinent too. It is that while it is helpful, because it throws a little light onto the dark side of the soul, to analyse the various sins and vices that afflict us all to varying degrees, it is not helpful to push that analysis beyond a certain point. The language of sin and vice is not a technical or forensic language. It is everyday language that can aid our introspection and observations and thereby enrich our self-understanding and inform the way we relate with others and take responsibility both personally and socially. Our effort here has not been to create a detailed and comprehensive map of the entire eco-system of the dark side of the soul. Such a task can, by definition, never be done. It's just too dark in there to be sure what's going on. Rather, the aim is to encourage growth in self-awareness in an area that is notoriously and necessarily difficult. Although same sin is straightforward, what taxes the introspective sinner is the complexity of their motives and the inter-connectedness of virtues as vices.

Our concern, therefore, has not been to work out what each of the seven deadly sins or the eight thoughts of Evagrius might mean in today's world. It has been to ask the more general question of how the idea that there really are deadly aspects of our soul, that the vices really are vicious, might take shape today. The starting point has thus been to think of the deadlies as ways in which we unwittingly undermine our own happiness, wellbeing and flourishing, together with the good and creative order of the communities in which we live. When, that is, we think of sins as problematic passions or as vices that make up the humid rainforest that is the dark side of our soul.

The result of exploring this question, incomplete and provisional as it necessarily is, has given shape to the six chapters that constitute the heart of this book. In some areas we have found ourselves mapping quite closely sins or thoughts that were established in the canon of the deadlies. We have looked at pride, sloth, envy, lust, greed and rage, and we began with gluttony. We departed from the tradition in two particularly important ways, however. First, in declining to make these traditional deadly sins 'capital', that is to see them as the fount of many other sins. It was the monk Cassian, the man who introduced Evagrius' scheme to the Latin-speaking Western world, who came up with the idea that the passions (which came to be called 'capitals') could have progeny (often called 'daughters'). My presentation here suggests not that there are capital sins and derivatives that can be arranged hierarchically, but that our vicious inclinations can be seen to cluster together in various ways. These clusters are not perhaps entirely stable, and different groupings may make sense from different perspectives or at different times. Nonetheless, it is important to cluster the vices, as the act of doing so is clarifying and because more is revealed about the nature of each vice when it is put alongside a small number of others. The second point of difference is that, following the lead of Judith Shklar, who herself was following Montaigne, I incorporate a range of 'ordinary vices' into the list of the deadlies. These draw on her list, but also range more widely. In particular I have sought to incorporate the insights about control from the work of Iain McGilchrist and to pick up on the increased narcissism of people today that is tracked and narrated by Jean Twenge.

What is offered here is not a reductionist account of human badness, unhappiness or evil, nor does it compete with scientific or medical explanations of some of the states, or with legal judgements regarding some of the behaviours that flow from them. It is an invitation to imagine the complex web of desires, anxieties, confusions and habits that make up the murky and opaque side of ourselves. Our sins and vices are not separate fountains of toxicity, but tangle together. This is a significant point, not only because it is a more truthful view of things, but also because it involves imagining the way sin and vice work within us very differently. The traditional system was splendid because it was an orderly hierarchy and therefore of great power and utility to those who would judge others and apply appropriate penalties and penances. It was also, as an organizing principle that could be caricatured and imagined in many different forms, a gift to literature and art. Yet ultimately it fails. As we saw in chapter 2, the attempt to write or read characters in stories in such a way as they manifest just one of the deadly sins is rarely going to be satisfactory. Yet that's not the reason why the Reformation era threw out the baby of imaginative connection with the bathwater of inappropriate theology. What was going on there is more adequately explained by the kind of argument that Iain McGilchrist puts forward and that we noted in chapter 7 – this was the tragic 'desire to control' moving into the ascendant and wanting to have things more organized, objective, precise and particular than is humanly realistic or helpful; a cultural manifestation of left-hemisphere functioning of which the Ten Commandments written upon boards or murals on church walls are an enduring visual aid.

The proposal here is to offer something that both captures a significant proportion of the truth about the way in which vice really does work within us to undermine us, and also to touch and inspire the creative imagination, whether that takes expression in verbal or non-verbal form. The hope is not that a new Dante will create a masterwork on the basis of the web of sin that stretches across the dark side of the soul. It's rather to give a framework that will encourage individual imaginations to be roused, and consciences inspired, to take responsibility not only for their best intentions and praiseworthy achievements, but also for the less flattering drivers of their thoughts, words and deeds. In particular, their lack of self-control, their vicious regards, their idealized ambitions, their demoralizing and in some cases deeply distorting confusions about time and money, their tragic desires and even their malicious tendencies. And to do this, despite the fact that, even on an enlightened day, they feel in the dark about much of this, and would love to attribute their faults, failings, mistakes and errors to objective causes just beyond the zone of personal responsibility, whether that be the power of suppressed memories, the bad influence of parents or peers, the unwanted intrusion of demon-whispered thoughts, the impact of internal chemical imbalance, or any other causes. In other words, the aim here has been to help people to connect the language of sin and vice with the issues that they confront in their hearts, lives, communities and cultures to aid introspection and guide mature responsibility taking.

Six Clusters of Vice

In the second chapter I offered a very brief overview of Evagrius' eight thoughts. Let me here offer a similarly audacious summary of the six clusters of vice that I have identified in the central chapters of this book.

Under the heading of 'Naughty, but nice' I have explored what self-indulgence looks like today. Even apparently benign things like talking or eating can, if indulged or allowed to get out of hand, begin to have harmful consequences that in the long run, and bearing in mind the impact on others as well as the self, will do considerably more harm than good. The way in which the Methodist Church has resolved to encourage its members to think about alcohol is offered as a suggestion of the sort of considerations that are relevant not only when we are concerned with intoxicants, but when we are engaging with anything where the pleasurable short-term rewards may prove to be distortingly attractive. The point is not to eliminate pleasure or enjoyment, but to militate against the easily overlooked but deleterious consequences of hostile pleasures or potentially problematic passions.

By 'vicious regards' I mean ways of looking at, thinking about, or otherwise appraising myself or others that are the opposite of 'kind' or 'respectful', and which have negative and damaging consequences. This is where I locate 'bad pride', a version of the sin that in the high Middle Ages was seen as the source of the others – human arrogant self-regard that leaves no room for God. As my scheme is not based on the idea of capitals but on that of a web, there is no attempt to relocate this sort of pride in a new position in a hierarchy – as there is no set hierarchy. Moreover it is plain that even the word 'pride' is too small and too limited to contain all the species of sin that are to do with the way we think ourselves up and others down. However, it is particularly important to recall that 'abjectness' is a form of vicious self-regard and that snobbery, vanity, status anxiety (a much more resonant phrase than 'vainglory' for most of us) and envy are potentially very toxic to ourselves and to our community and society.

Any thought concerning the ethical ideals and spiritual aspirations that people harbour about themselves today needs to bear in mind the extraordinary weight that is placed on integrity as a value. Sadly this often puts an impossible ideal in front of people and so sets us all up to fail. It is perhaps for this reason that we have such strong feelings about hypocrisy – feelings that are connected with defensiveness. Knowing ourselves to be hypocritical when judged by the ideals of integrity, we redouble our efforts to keep this truth from our many critics out there as well as from ourselves. The desire for certainty, and the fantasy of perfectionism, both fuelled by narcissism, itself part of the eco-system of the dark side of the soul, are all part of this particularly and ironically self-defeating cluster of vices that have in common their out-of-control idealism.

Quite how to handle the legacy of the notion of 'acedia' is a question that has puzzled many thinkers down the centuries. Some see it as a concept that predated melancholy, which is the forebear of depression – itself a very difficult concept to handle, blurring as it so easily can the distinctions between experiences that are healthy responses to circumstances with a condition with neurophysiological or historic causes. Another version of the acedia story is that it is more connected with the even fuzzier and internally diverse experience of boredom. Then again, there are words like good old guilt-inspiring 'sloth' or 'laziness' within this especially misty word-cloud. I have taken a slightly different approach, and seen acedia as a cluster of issues that derive from our problems with *time*, for centuries a puzzle to philosophers, and more recently to physicists and psychologists. The truth is that time is more complex, especially psychologically and spiritually, than we often register. By 'temporal disjunctions' I mean to refer to those negative consequences of not having a good relationship with time – time not being mere *chronos* but sometimes, at least, as complex as the weather, or possibly another person. And so I cluster together sloth (failing to connect constructively and responsibly with the present moment) and boredom (the sense that time has stopped) and vicious busyness (which is based on the idea that we are running out of time), and also nostalgia (a word I deliberately *misuse* to mean a bad relationship with the past, *or the future, or the present moment*, or, just as likely, all three). Being in a muddle about time, out of synch with time, is the cause of real distress, endless errors and much misery. By recognizing a vicious cluster here we might begin to take responsibility for the temporal nature, patterns and rhythms of our own lives and those of our communities.

To talk about 'tragic desires' brings us back to more familiar sin-like territory. However, whereas the Christian tradition has for many centuries brought lust into the limelight, this exploration has deliberately drawn more attention to the prim desire to control than to unrefined lasciviousness. Love of money and a more general insatiability are also in this cluster. These desires are all tragic because they cannot and will not be fulfilled. Lust is the misuse of attention, distracting us from the care and maintenance of relationships that are integral to true and long-term love. Avarice is love of money, which of all things is the most unlikely to return the favour because it is either inert or abstract. Insatiability is, by definition, chronic unfulfilment. Insatiability is tragic because we do not realize what it is driving us and our economy, and therefore ecology, towards, while control is tragic not because there is no controlling to be done, but because the desire to control routinely overestimates its capacity and its place in a wise and virtuous person or community.

Finally we come to our 'malicious tendencies' – in particular, cruelty, spite, rage and revenge. Of these, only rage is a traditional deadly, and yet cruelty and spite and the apparently motiveless and unrewarding acts that hurt others are a significant and puzzling part of what people do. That we can't answer the 'why question' about these acts need not perturb us particularly, for our premise is that there is in us much we don't know, a good deal we can't sort out, and a fair bit we will never control; yet it is all part of who we are, and we only diminish ourselves yet further by not taking responsibility. To take responsibility for one's own unwitting nastinesses is counter-intuitive, but only because we have, whatever else we may persuade ourselves of, taken on board the guilt- and blame-inflicting elements of traditional ways of sin-based moralizing, and thrown away the creative, insightful and therapeutic aspects of trying to take responsibility for our whole selves, not only warts and all, but web of sin and all.

What we have, then, is a tentative picture, imaginatively constructed, on the basis of many different kinds of evidence and argument, insight and intuition. It doesn't pretend to be the last word about anything, but it does add up to an argument that the word 'sin' is neither a laughing matter nor yet adequately described, especially when it is focused on culinary self-indulgence or sexual desire or expression. *Sin*, as understood here, is *vicious*, as understood here. That it is also murky is not a reason to leave it to its own devices while we seek to deal with issues that are less intractable and that help excuse us of that most fundamental human dignity and sacrifice: to take responsibility for things that we neither fully understand nor are capable of entirely controlling.

10

Demon Wrestling:
A Practical Guide

I have been suggesting that there is a 'dark side' to every human being and that it can be helpfully imagined as a web of interconnecting sins and vices. Because our awareness of this web is at best limited, these sins and vices, while actually part of who we are, can often seem to act on us from outside ourselves, and are indeed able to circumvent or override our conscious will. This creates a dilemma. What can we do about those aspects of ourselves that are negative and destructive but also murky and mysterious to us? There are two possible answers. One is that we capitulate to them. The other is that we wrestle with them. This chapter explores option two and asks what is involved in wrestling with our demons.

If we are to set out to wrestle with these demons with any kind of confidence we must bear in mind the image of the web of sin. It would be all too easy to make matters worse by struggling in an anxious, panicky or disorganized way. And so, despite the assumption that we are fighting more or less blind here, it is helpful to name the demons.

In particular, to name the ones we feel attack us most profoundly or regularly, or, if you prefer a different idiom, those of our vices that are most vicious.

Naming demons, sins and vices is a way of robbing them of some of their power, but also of claiming back some personal responsibility. Nonetheless, it's a more difficult exercise than it might at first sight seem. And even when we have named and shamed some of our tendencies we can still be lulled into complacency. 'My avarice is so powerful that I really am the boy (or girl) who simply *has* to have it all.' 'My acedia is such an important part of who I am that it is unreasonable to expect me to pull my weight.' Nonetheless, it is reasonable to hope that freshening up the language of vice might help us to avoid some of the choices and habits that in the end do us and others more harm than good. That it might help us deal with temptation.

Our analysis so far has enabled us to name two dozen or so different sins or vices and group them into six clusters. We have noted that, in the past, different people have identified different sins as the most serious or the origin of others, going back to St Paul, for whom 'the love of money is the root of all kinds of evil', to the tradition that put pride at the top of the list, and those who, like Evagrius, saw acedia as especially problematic. To this list we might add the Augustinian concern with lack of self-control connected with lust. Asking what contemporary authors bring to the party we have seen how 'narcissism', 'envy', 'cruelty', 'control' and 'insatiability' are also proper causes of very serious concern. We noted in passing that the archaic-sounding 'vainglory' is very closely related to what today is more comfortably thought of as 'status anxiety' – inappropriate concern about how others regard us. This may seem like an entry-level sin, a junior demon, but it is capable of causing terrible havoc though many micro-interventions that between them replace the value of excellence with that of performance, and the desire to be of service with the desire to be seen.

Trying to identify, name, and to a degree understand the demons that beset us from the dark side of our soul, has been the main task of the central chapters of this book. It is admittedly (and inevitably) incomplete, and serious demon wrestlers might be challenged to identify a few more that are lurking semi-hidden on the dark side of their own soul. It is shockingly easy, once you get the hang of it, to find fault with oneself. However, to continue on and on in that vein is yet another form of self-indulgence and vanity. The question of what, if anything, can be done about these aspects of who we are – these sins, vices and demons – is one that has been of concern to many down the centuries, and it is right that we should give it some attention, even if we have a feeling that we are never going to achieve a decisive victory. To do that, we need first to reflect a little more on the diverse reality of temptation.

Types of Temptation

When, during the Second World War, C. S. Lewis wrote *The Screwtape Letters* he explored what temptation looked like for someone newly converted to Christianity. He did it by imagining the way in which the senior devil, Screwtape, might mentor the junior devil, Wormwood, who had been sent to tempt and taunt the new convert and ultimately distract him from the joy and peace of God. As Screwtape puts it to Wormwood, 'you are there to fuddle him'. He expounds his strategy more fully in the sixth letter, in which Screwtape says how conducive uncertainty about the future is from his diabolical perspective (from which 'the Enemy' is God).

> We want him to be in the maximum uncertainty, so that his mind will be filled with contradictory pictures of the future, every one of which arouses hope or fear. There is nothing like suspense and anxiety for barricading a human's mind against the Enemy. He wants men to be concerned with what they do; our business is to keep them thinking about what will happen to them.

The merit of *The Screwtape Letters* is not in the novelty of its spiritual advice, but in the accessible, creative and witty way in which it is presented (a method that we might now identify as appealing to the right hemisphere of the brain). Nonetheless, Lewis does offer us also a more subtle understanding of temptation than we might naturally bring to the word. Temptation here is not merely the desire to do something that is forbidden, or to break a rule or a law, or to transgress a boundary. It is to be driven by anxiety or to allow one's consciousness to be dominated by uncertainty. Temptation, in other words, is taken out of the 'naughty, but nice' territory and is grounded in the theological notion that God desires human freedom and flourishing. The contrary, demonic, purpose is that people should lose their freedom in anxiety, petty concerns and fragmentation. So Screwtape writes: 'We want to suck in, He [God] wants to give out. We are empty and would be filled; He is full and flows over. Our war aim is a world in which Our Father Below [the devil] has drawn all other beings into himself: the Enemy [God] wants a world full of beings united to Him but still distinct.'

When it comes to wrestling with demons, struggling without getting further entangled in the web of sin and vice, it is important also to recognize the asymmetrical nature of virtue and vice. 'We', writes Screwtape,

> can drag our patients along by continual tempting, because we design them only for the table, and the more their will is interfered with the better. He cannot 'tempt' to virtue as we do to vice. He wants them to learn to walk and must therefore take away His hand; and if only the will to walk is really there He is pleased even with their stumbles.

What all this means is that temptation needs to be understood not as desire that makes us feel guilty, but as inclination to get entrapped in that which is harmful to us and which inhibits our flourishing and our freedom. The 'demons' that we have to wrestle with are those aspects of who we are that diminish and fragment our being, leaving us not only unhappy but also unfree.

Not that demons present themselves like this. The vices and sins, to continue to speak metaphorically, do not honestly present the consequences of succumbing to them. Rather they emphasize short-term and obvious rewards, and promise the release from the pressure to learn, to grow or to accommodate to others that is integral to human life. Lewis is right to point to the power of the temptation that many experience, when faced with an uncertain future, to speculate about it and to become absorbed by their own fantasies – whether positive or negative, hopes or fears – rather than to engage with the realities at hand. Anxious uncertainty is one of the drivers of 'temporal disjunction'. Fuddled by the future, we find that our relationship with the past and the present start to go awry. But it is not the only consequence. Anxious uncertainty also aggravates our inner control freak, and so we find ourselves desiring more control and seeking more certainty than is realistic or feasible. That these hopeless desires are frustrated, as they inevitably are, by no means sobers us into a careful recalibration of what is possible based on a realistic understanding of our actual limits. Rather the frustration irritates and annoys us, goading us to more strenuous and urgent, yet also increasingly petty, and ultimately futile, attempts to gain certainty and exercise control over the future. All this has the tragic consequence not only of failing to control the future, but of failing to perceive the delights, opportunities and responsibilities that are alive in the present moment. As the demon Screwtape says to Wormwood, 'nearly all vices are rooted in the future. Gratitude looks to the past and love to the present; fear, avarice, lust, and ambition look ahead.' Later he explains his aim.

But we want a man hag-ridden by the Future – haunted by visions of an imminent heaven or hell upon earth – ready to break the Enemy's commands in the present if by doing so we make him think he can attain the one or aver the other – dependent for his faith on the success or failure of schemes whose end he will not live to see. We want a whole race perpetually in pursuit of the rainbow's end, never honest, nor kind, nor happy *now*, but always using as mere fuel wherewith to heap the altar of the future every real gift which is offered them in the Present.

This, expressed in the language of the twenty-first century, is the temptation to be *busy*. As we have seen, it is a common and contemporary, if paradoxical, form of acedia. Yet it is not accompanied by shame or guilt. Rather it is a source of narcissistic pride, self-importance, and, as it is usually *performed*, it is directly connected with vainglory or status anxiety, and it is often entered into with just that sort of certainty that diminishes the possibility of self-awareness to vanishing point for as long as the sinful episode persists. Moreover, as we saw earlier, it is the nature of vicious busyness to be *chronic*. And so it is that, if we were to stop for a moment and listen carefully, we might hear the dry cackles of Screwtape and his minions when we draw up our endless to-do lists and check our emails at bedtime.

We have emphasized throughout this book the darkness of the dark side of the soul, and the invisibility of the web of sin. This worked example of busyness allows us to appreciate another truth about that darkness. It's not just the lack of illumination; it's the effectiveness of the disguise. All metaphors break down sooner or later, and whereas the dark side of the moon is the ever-changing area that we cannot see because it is facing away from us, the dark side of the soul is sometimes invisible because the filaments of the web of sin are so thin, and sometimes because vices have learnt how to disguise themselves as virtues, and sometimes because the darkness is so deep we can't believe there is anything there. All this makes temptation very difficult to spot, and makes it likely that it is just as we venture out in high-minded style and with virtuous intent that we fall into some unseen but vicious trap. There is another problem too, in that we often expect to find temptation in the wrong place.

We imagine it to conform with our idea of the seedy, the disreputable and the ugly, and so we miss its brightly illuminated and audaciously brazen presence, not only right in front of our noses, but on our vaingloriously boasting lips, in our viciously regarding eyes and in our censoriously wagging or meanly pointing finger.

This is another reason why seeing sin through the lens of self-indulgence or wilful transgression is so inadequate. There are times when this is precisely what is going on. Drinking ourselves to oblivion, desiring another's spouse, gossiping malicious half-truths, abusing the trust invested in us on account of our position of power in the community or at work, not bothering to do our share of the domestic chores or to care adequately for vulnerable family members at home . . . none of this is commendable, all of it is wrong, and, depending on all sorts of factors, we will capitulate to these and the myriad similar temptations and derogations of the path of virtue more or less frequently. But we can hardly say of these that we really didn't know what we were doing, even if we can accurately say that even as we were doing them we were anguished and torn apart within – both wanting to and wanting not to at the same time.

There are, then, three forms of temptation relating to three types of vice. First, there are the temptations to engage in vices that look like vices and which we are either going to resist because they are so plainly flagged or going to engage in wholeheartedly, knowing that this is the road to hell, but hey, who cares. Second, there are temptations to engage in the vices that look like vices and which we engage in with very mixed feelings and regret even as we participate. And third, there are the vices that look like virtues and which we engage in because we are deeply deluded about the nature of true virtue.

The idea of wrestling with our demons fits most easily with 'Type-two' temptations, but these are not necessarily the most dangerous, damaging or toxic. The worst things are those that have managed to disguise themselves in the clothes of social acceptability or even virtue; not only do we neglect to fight or resist them, but we think that to do so is wrong. We are not aware of any temptation when we engage in vices disguised as virtues because we long ago succumbed to the temptation to a stealth-like form of acedia that caused us to neglect to reflect adequately on what we suppose to be good. Our tactics for demon wrestling therefore need to be aware of this and incorporate proactive as well as reactive strategies. But before considering how we might fight our demons today, let's see what Evagrius advised in the fourth century.

Answering Back

When asked to compose a treatise that would help his fellow hermits cope with demons in the desert, Evagrius wrote a book called *Antirrheticus* or, as it has been imaginatively translated, *Talking Back*. This follows the method that the Bible tells us Jesus used when tempted by Satan in the wilderness of quoting back an apposite verse of Scripture to shut him up. Satan famously gave up on Jesus after three attempts. Evagrius had more of a fight, and, anticipating the worst for his fellow hermits, lists 498 thoughts and adduces a short passage from the Bible to address each one. While many of the connections he makes between a thought and Scripture might strike us as curious, there are some that sound a more resonant note. Whether or not we believe that words of the Bible have supernatural demon-slaying powers, the introspective analysis and honesty that offers such a panoply of troubling thoughts is itself impressive and instructive. Consider these examples, which concern the love of money.

> Against the thought that did not permit us to give to a needy brother who asked to borrow something from us: 'You shall not close your hand to your brother who is in need. You shall open your hands to him and lend him as much as he needs.'
>
> Against the thought that seeks to keep resources for itself and does not want to give relief to one of the brothers from them: 'Cursed shall be your barns and your reserves. Cursed shall be the offspring of your belly and the fruits of your land.'
>
> Against the soul that clings to the world, loves temporal things, and wants the house and property of its parents: 'Listen daughter, and see, and incline your ear: forget your people and your father's house. For the King has desired your beauty.'

He finds similar messages in the New Testament.

> Against the inner thoughts that want to acquire riches and to consume the intellect with anxiety about them: 'Do not store up for yourselves treasures on earth, where moth and rust consume and where thieves break in and steal.'
>
> Against the thoughts of love of money that corrupt kindness to the brothers: 'And be kind to one another, tenderhearted, forgiving one another, as God in Christ as forgiven you.'

Evagrius has here identified the sort of inner trouble that people of any era might experience: a hesitancy to lend, compassion fatigue, inheritance anxiety, the failure to realize that material things all need to be looked after and so create work and stress even as we acquire them, and the observation that our insatiable avarice also makes us unkind.

When it comes to addressing the thought of anger the following are among his sixty-four suggestions.

Against the thought that is stirred up by anger and wants to revile the brothers: 'You shall abstain from every unjust word.'

Against the thought that is quickly aroused by anger and, based on a trivial pretext, agitates the intellect: 'A fool immediately announces his anger, but a clever man conceals his disgrace.'

And the slightly more subtle:

Against the thought of anger that prevents us from answering with humility those who chastise us rightly: 'Anger destroys even wise persons; a submissive answer turns away anger, but a painful word raises up anger.'

Against the thought that provokes us to strife with the brothers and prevents us from cutting off arguments: 'An irascible man prepares arguments, but a patient one soothes an argument that is just starting.'

Although Evagrius' major concern about anger is that it is deeply unsettling to prayer, we can see in even these few examples that he identifies something of the range of the danger of irascibility: the desire to 'revile' – that is to criticize insultingly, or to lambast with such great hostility that the desire for the hurtful word takes over from the attempt to be honest; basing anger on trivial pretexts, which suggests that the provocation was perhaps sought, or at least the result of an ungenerous reading of a situation or comment; the failure to respond with humility; and, in the fourth example, failure at a later stage in an angry conflict actively to seek to cool it down.

Intriguing as it would be to examine Evagrius' ideas for 'answering back' to all eight of his 'thoughts', we will content ourselves with just three – the third being vainglory, where one example will suffice. It is a salutary one for those who write as well as those who teach, and indeed all who would advise others.

> Against the thought of vainglory that encourages us to teach although we have not acquired the soul's health or knowledge of the truth: 'Not many of you should become teachers, my brothers, for you know that we who teach will be judged with greater strictness. For all of us make many mistakes. Anyone who makes no mistakes in speaking is perfect, able to keep the whole body in check with a bridle.'

The approach I am taking here is that, as far as human beings are concerned, 'all have sinned', all are more familiar with the vices than they would like to be or generally admit, and none has totally dealt with all the demons and thoughts that trouble them. This reframes the whole notion of what it is to teach, advise or counsel. It's not about those who know informing those who don't know, but about those who have explored the murk reporting back the results, as best they can articulate them, of scouting around in the dark. Nonetheless, Evagrius can, as usual, point us to a helpful insight.

It's all too easy to forget one's own faults and failings when advising others how to be good.

Seven Tactics for Demon Wrestling

People have been wrestling demons for a long time. Jesus set about it by fasting and praying in the wilderness for forty days and forty nights and then answering back decisively. Evagrius fasted and prayed for far longer and found that no sooner had one demon been answered than another one plopped a slightly different and perhaps even more beguiling thought into his head. As a result, he produced his list of almost five hundred biblical 'answers'. It is a daunting list, but it scarcely seems adequate to today's world of myriad temptations, some of which are obvious, some of which seem irresistible – though failing to resist causes us shame and anguish – and many of which are invisible to us.

The deadly sin tradition that developed from Pope Gregory's appropriation and adaptation of Evagrius' thoughts tended to espouse the view that contraries cure contraries. This is the idea that cultivating virtue is the way to deal with vice. Thus humility is put forward as the remedy for pride, generosity as the answer to avarice, joy the antidote to envy and so on. As a way of wrestling with demons this has an obvious, if not tautological, strength, especially if translated to the simpler and more behavioural vices. If the talkative talk less then they will have dealt, to a degree, with the problem. What the talkative need to learn, however, is *how* to talk less. They need to learn the skill of biting the tongue, or to acquire a little restraint when it comes to proffering their opinions. That question is not convincingly addressed by the injunction to talk less or even the personal resolution to do so. This is even more extremely the case with more complex vices like envy, even though it strikes us as intuitively correct that the joyful have little room for envy, and logically correct that joyfulness is a very different spirit to envy.

Nonetheless, many would be able to think of the occasions when a sunny day of positive personal wellbeing and happiness was marred by a cloud of envy (or lust or avarice, perhaps) passing across the sky for no good or justifiable reason. Such unbidden, spoiling vices are not amenable to the contrary treatment, unless we are very quick about our cognitive and spiritual business. A better tactic is to seek habits of mind and life, or spiritual or ethical ambitions, that make it less likely for the cloud to form in the first place.

Nonetheless, when we are enveloped by envy, remembering our reasons to be positive, grateful and joyful can be a very helpful step. This is how a contrary can cure. It is certainly better than wallowing in our envy or taking some action based on it. Unless perhaps that action is to look to our laurels and try a bit harder, in which case our envy has been transformed from vicious to virtuous. The contrary virtue is something to look for when we are aware of the presence of a vice in us, or when we realize that we are coming under the sway of one of our demons. There can be few wiser things to do than this, and yet knowing what the contrary virtue is, and knowing how to attain it, can be far from simple.

This is especially so when it comes to the acedic vices, like apathy, boredom and so on, and it is the failure to understand what the contrary actually *is* that lies behind the observation that busyness too is an acedic vice. These matters are rarely straightforward. The avaricious are not necessarily cured of their financial greed by making generous donations, as we have seen. Something of insatiability persists, and the excessive desire to control that has had such an important role in driving the success that has made the avaricious person wealthy remains, as does the vainglory or status anxiety that fuels the need for 'donor recognition'. Development professionals who use such terms will assure us that they are dealing with human nature in the best interests of achieving a good income stream from 'major donors'. This may be true, but looked at from the perspective being developed here, we might see it as a way of working with the dark side of the soul that leaves the demons relatively untroubled. That's a pragmatic approach, but we shall have to try harder than that if we believe that the way of vice truly is vicious, both in terms of making people unhappy and in undermining the common good.

We really do need to know what to do in the face of all these temptations, vices, demons and sins. It is unhelpful to say that we must just be vigilant against them all, and naïve to imagine that there is one simple antidote, or that we can regularly summon up the appropriate 'contrary'. The biblical example of fasting and prayer might commend itself when dealing with what seems to be an incorrigible inclination to fall for one particular temptation, or generally to find demonic whispering persuasive, only to regret it deeply sometime later, if not immediately afterwards. The petition 'Lead us not into temptation' has pride of penultimate place in the Lord's Prayer – just before the earnest prayer to be delivered from evil. The lively pray-er might want to rephrase it in their mind, asking for the wisdom to understand what really is a temptation, to identify the distinctively seductive tones of a demonic voice in the imagination, or be able to see from a distance the viciousness of vice and at least try to take evasive action and avoid the attractions that will prove in time to have been nothing more than a trap – an escape from happiness, not a step into it.

As we have seen, one of the issues that demon wrestlers face today is that they live in a culture where sin is not taken to be a serious matter of spirituality. What is vital, therefore, is to recognize that sin *is* a spiritual issue, even when understood in the more secular language of a vice, and to consider adopting some sort of spiritual tactic with the express intention of identifying temptation accurately and being confident enough to say, 'No, I have decided not to do think or feel that.'

The first two tactics in demon wrestling are, then, to *recognize that sin is a serious spiritual issue*, and to *develop spiritual assertiveness*. This second one won't always be possible, but neither will anything else.

A number of vices and sins are rooted in *excesses of appetite*. Some of these are entirely natural and, when looked at scientifically, adaptive. There are a million ways of dealing with excesses of appetite, ranging from Alcoholics Anonymous and its derivatives, to Weight Watchers and a thousand other dietary programmes. One thing these organizations have taught us is that demon wrestling is better done in the company of others. Not only is egocentric narcissism a major contemporary vice, but it is a vice that makes it harder for us to deal with other quite different vices, because it tempts us to see ourselves as so singular, special, unique that we have nothing to learn from others. This is a big mistake.

So the third tactic in demon wrestling is to *learn from others*. Seek out the company of those who have already gone a few rounds, and learn a few moves from them.

The notion that the self is simply an isolated, individual, 'me', is a corrosive distortion of reality that has many consequences, depending on how far we let it corrupt us. It is such thinking that makes us prey to the temptations of pride and vainglory, but also to abjectness and envy. Such distortions also feed into the vices clustered together as impossible ideals and tragic desires. This is the distortion of *self-idolatry* or excessive narcissism. We get caught up with this when we lack humility – and lacking humility is a very common problem today because many people have not had the advantage of anyone ever trying to help them learn it, on account of the fact that humility is not held in high regard these days, though, as we have seen, it is increasingly on the agenda for those in positions of responsibility that involve the leadership of others. Provided the virtue of humility is properly distinguished from the vice of abjectness, there is no reason to be suspicious of the pathway that aspiring to humility opens up for us.

But learning humility is not easy. Taking up 'humility' as a New Year's Resolution is never going to get anyone very far. Nonetheless, if we engage with the matter with due spiritual seriousness it is possible to learn humility and to learn it intentionally. Indeed, this is exactly the decision that Jorge Mario Bergoglio took at some point in his life between being removed from office as leader of the Jesuits of Argentina and becoming the first Pope Francis. As Paul Vallely has argued, 'humility was more like an intellectual stance than a personal temperament—a tool he developed in his struggle against what he had learned were the weaknesses in his own personality, with its rigid, authoritarian, and egotistical streaks'.

So we are in good company when we adopt the fourth tactic in dealing with demons, which is to *seek humility*.

As learning humility is both intrinsically difficult, and something that few people set as a life-goal, a few pointers might be appropriate. Here are two possible ways to get started. The first is to attend to your mistakes, especially mistakes that are the result of the sorts of vices and sins that we have been considering here. Not the overtly guilt-inducing ones or manifestly ugly ones, but the ones that we have engaged in when and sometimes precisely because we were sure we were doing the right thing. The second way to learn humility is the more risky strategy of so failing to attend to your mistakes and errors, and the way in which you distress and alienate others, that you end up in a terrible mess and hit rock bottom. This is the easier method, but it is much riskier, as people don't always bounce back after such falls. The way to think about this is not in terms of the mess people get into through untreated addiction, sad though that is. Think rather about what happens to those who grow accustomed to abusing their power. The tragedy of this vice is that no one tells people who are abusing their power that they are doing so until it gets to the point that their power is going to be, or is, removed. Then are the mighty both fallen and isolated. But there is an alternative: start to learn humility now. Or at least make humility a positive word in your vocabulary and a personal, if long-term, aspiration.

It is clear from chapter 6 that we need a tactic that can begin to address the extraordinarily powerful cluster of *temporal disjunctions* that reflect the ancient idea of acedia. It's the problem of 'not bothering', or 'not caring', or, rather, 'not caring as we would if we had a good and healthy relationship with time and purpose, together with a mature and settled sense of our responsibilities and potential – and indeed our limits'. This is *not* the temptation not to make an effort; indeed, when this vice traps us our exertions may become excessive. It is rather the temptation to act as if there is no purpose or accountability. Acedia is the vice of having lost the plot – 'plot' here meaning a combination of purpose and time. As such it does great damage on its own, and also interacts ferociously (if imperceptibly) with the others.

Combating acedia, like combating self-idolatry, is best done preventatively. Once the demon gets you, whether at noonday or in the small hours of the night, you are in trouble. But it is not easy or straightforward to describe precisely those tactics and habits that will ward off an attack. It would be easy to suggest that to ward off acedia we need to learn a thoroughgoing life wisdom, and that is certainly the 'contrary' that is needed. But to say this is little more than to state the problem in reverse. It is more helpful to suggest that what is needed here is 'time wisdom'. Time wisdom is not the same as 'time management'; for one thing, those with excellent time-management skills can often end up super-busy – a happy enough state until it starts to become a way of life: then it becomes the vicious busyness that we discussed in chapter 6. Time wisdom is a combination of insights into the nature of time, self-awareness and a sense of what makes life – and therefore the experience of time – worthwhile.

The best way to deal with acedia is to *pursue time wisdom*. Ultimately, time wisdom delivers a confidence that time has a shape and purpose and that there is a time for everything. Such a project is a serious and long-term one. Putting it alongside the tactic of aspiring to humility makes it seem especially daunting. So, while honouring the big point about generally pursuing a wise approach to time, the actual particular tactic that might be used to combat acedia is simply this: *set goals.*

Goal setting is helpful because it begins to give a texture to time. Imagine playing football without there being a goal. It would be fun for a while but, without point or purpose, everyone would begin to flag, as indeed they would if on a long hike with no destination in mind. Goal setting deals with the problem that time feels too long, that it seems to stand still. Goal setting in this sense is very different to being given a target by someone else, as it is not part of being managed or challenged by others, but of taking responsibility. Athletes do it all the time, especially when they are, as it were, battling against themselves; as we are when we are wrestling with our demons. Goals do not need to be achieved; their purpose is to help shape purpose and time, not to guarantee success.

Goals can and should be revised. And goals can be modest, and set in the interest of others. Negative goals are also potentially very helpful. You could think of Sabbath keeping as a negative goal – the purposeful intention of doing no work so that natural processes of recovery and restoration can take place. It is very different to keep the Sabbath as a matter of obedience than as a matter of personal resolve and intention. When the latter happens the negative begins to become positive as a set of Sabbath-values emerges to make sense of investing time in activities that don't immediately seem worthwhile, and one discovers some of the true (i.e. non-avaricious) richness of life. Goal setting can and should also be positive and directly life-giving. There is no reason why someone should not set a goal of spending more time with friends, or engaging with the arts, or in physical exercise or spiritual practices. To do so might be a proactive form of demon wrestling.

The problem with goal setting is that it can get out of hand. The control freak that is lurking in the left hemisphere of your brain just loves the sounds of these suggestions and can't wait to get cracking by grasping the pen or setting up a spreadsheet to list and monitor all your goals. That is indeed a danger, and it is why it is appropriate to see goal setting in the context of the pursuit of time wisdom, and acedia in the context of the other clusters of vice, and the literally endless sources of temptation that beset us.

The fifth tactic, then, is to *set time-wise and realistic goals*.

Sixth, we need some sort of strategy for dealing with the fundamentally *unhealthy attitudes* that are involved in a number of the sins and vices. While it is tempting to distinguish between attitudes towards the self and attitudes towards others, our insistence throughout this book that the self is itself relational means that this distinction ultimately breaks down, and suggests that negative, misjudged and hurtful attitudes will have consequences on both self and others that are deeply entwined, if not indistinguishable.

The underlying issue here is the strange attraction of *not* loving either self or others, and the tactic needed is to learn how to love. Christianity has always considered love to have four possible objects: God, other people (aka neighbours), yourself and your enemies. It has also seen these loves as profoundly interconnected – 'love your neighbour as yourself'. Love is also to be an activity that involves the complete dedication of the whole person, so that God, for instance, must be loved 'with all thy heart, with all thy mind, with all thy soul and with all thy strength'. Learning to love, comprehensively and truly, is a surprisingly positive way of dealing with our demons. It involves turning away from the avaricious tentacles of self and replacing complex and muddled vicious regards with simple loving attention. It may not be easy, but it is extremely positive to deal with our demons not by worrying about them but by doing what we can to love others – neighbours and enemies – and to develop an attitude towards both ourselves and God which can also be called loving.

The sixth tactic in demon wrestling, then, is to *learn to love*.

And connected with this is the seventh and final tactic. Although negative, this is a tactic of singular importance. As we have seen, a number of vices develop when people try to love things that are not love-worthy and are not capable of reciprocating. Money is the most obvious example, but there are more than hints of similar distortions underlying lust and control and narcissism. The final tactic is therefore to identify things that attract us, and which draw from us a response and a desire that is very like love, and to understand that while these things matter, they are actually not worthy of love, because they cannot reciprocate.

The seventh tactic in demon wrestling is to *identify what is not love-worthy*.

Epilogue:
All Shall Be Well

The twentieth century has seen many advances in the understanding of human distress and its treatment. The various talking and humanistic cures ranging from psychoanalysis to therapy to counselling to a spot of Cognitive Behavioural Therapy (CBT), and now Mindfulness training, are deeply embedded in our culture. They exist alongside medical approaches that are increasingly used for people with anxiety or depression – conditions that have fuzzy boundaries with the more everyday experiences of those who have no cause to believe that a medical diagnosis is appropriate. Clearly there are some for whom a medical practitioner or therapist should and will be an early port of call. But increasingly widely needed as such support is, no one argues that each and every human being has a mental health issue that requires such professional attention. However, the argument here is that each and every person does have a dark side to their soul. We all have our demons, and we are on our own with them precisely because they are part of who we are. We can't escape. To excuse ourselves is futile. There seems to be no alternative to some kind of spiritual struggle; some sort of wrestling with our demons.

Such fighting will largely be a matter of scrapping in the dark, as if we are blindfolded. No wonder we long for the enlightenment that therapy might promise – to understand where it all comes from and therefore be able to deal with it. And yet Kathleen Norris, who writes so compellingly about the borderlands between depression and acedia, wonders whether the serenity and joy of Julian of Norwich should really, if taken absolutely seriously, be 'the end of all our therapies and potions'. Julian, like Evagrius, was a hermit who pondered deeply in her little cell – during the late fourteenth and early fifteenth century – about why it was that sin should be in the world. Her prayer and fasting was rewarded with 'shewings' or 'revelations' which caused her to write that 'all shall be well, and all shall be well, and all manner of thing shall be well'. I don't read Norris as decrying the benefits of therapeutic interventions; rather, as pointing out their limits. As she explains from her own experience,

> Although I was helped by a Jungian analyst when I was in my early twenties, and my husband and I benefitted on several occasions from marriage counseling, I have found therapy to be of limited usefulness, constrained in ways that religion is not, because it consistently falls short of mystery, by which I mean a profound simplicity that allows for paradox and poetry. In therapy I am likely to be searching for explanations, causes, and definitions, information that will help me change my behavior in healthful ways. But wisdom is the goal of spiritual seeking, as it is religion's true home.

Words like 'poetry' and 'paradox' are at the heart of what is at stake here. Whether today we instantly connect them with 'religion', and whether we connect any of this with 'wisdom' is another matter. If Iain McGilchrist, whose ideas about the divided brain we encountered when thinking about 'control', is right in his reading of the historical story through which we have come to our contemporary cultural environment, it is likely that we will see disconnects here, rather than a healthy set of connections or even a mysterious whole. The way in which he describes the cultural impact of the Reformation, which, as we have noted, largely superseded the tradition of understanding ourselves though the lens of the deadlies and replaced it with the prohibiting Ten Commandments, is telling and important. For McGilchrist it is a decisive 'slide into the territory of the left hemisphere'. The elements of this include:

> The preference for what is clear and certain over what is ambiguous or undecided; the preference for what is single, fixed, static and systematised, over what is multiple, fluid, moving and contingent; the emphasis on the word over the image, on literal meaning in language over metaphorical meaning, and the tendency for language to refer to other written texts or explicit meanings, rather than, through the cracks in language, if one can put it that way, to something Other beyond; the tendency towards abstraction, coupled with a downgrading of the realm of the physical; a concern with re-presentation rather than with presentation; in its more puritanical elements, an attack on music; the deliberate attempt to do away with the past and the contextually modulated, implicit wisdom of a tradition, replacing it with a new, rational, explicit, but fundamentally secular, order; and an attack on the sacred that was vehement in the extreme, and involved repeated and violent acts of desecration.

One doesn't need to agree with every detail of McGilchrist's argument to accept that there is a strong case for reviewing the priority we give the left hemisphere's mode of paying attention. It has its place, but it is not the first or last or whole story. We need to be able to reflect on the murky and troublesome aspects of who we are and what we experience in language, metaphor and image that encourage responsibility by resisting both reductionism and determinism. We need to do this in the name of both personal dignity and decent community; that is, in the name of the responsible, relational self.

The seven tactics for demon wrestling that I have suggested offer a few starting points, but they do not guarantee 'success'. There is no end to spiritual struggle. We cannot kill all our demons; we can't eradicate all our vices, resist all temptation, or desist from all our sins. Part of who we are will always remain mysteriously murky to us, and we will doubtless remain at least something of an irritation to our families and friends – even if we ourselves can't really see why, believing all our thoughts, words and deeds to be either perfectly reasonable or entirely excusable. But all have sinned, and all will sin; all have vices, and most of us are more tangled in the web of sin than we begin to appreciate until we think with a shiver how history might judge us, or how anyone might judge us if they knew us as well as we know ourselves – recognizing that even that leaves out the really dark stuff that still hides beyond the horizon of self-awareness. If we believe in God we need to believe in a forgiving God; and if we don't believe in God, we need to learn how to forgive ourselves.

Evagrius found a way through all this and was in the end known by his fellow monks not as a terrifying spiritual warrior but as a gentle and peaceable soul, showing many fruits in his life of his inner peaceableness. As Kathleen Norris puts it, 'this was a man who did not allow the bitter circumstances of his life to make *him* bitter'. This is not about 'superior spiritual accomplishment' but about coming to the sort of flourishing that allows and enables others to come to their fulfilment and that thereby builds and sustains community. These may seem modest aims indeed, but, as Jesus famously said of small children, 'of such is the kingdom of heaven'. Such modest aims, our 'tactics for demon wrestling', boil down to a little spiritual assertiveness, some genuine time wisdom, aspiring to humility and learning how to love that which is worth loving. Such is the path towards wisdom on which we find ourselves if we take sin seriously and begin to appreciate the viciousness of vice. Nothing could be further from the guilt-trip that the popular imagination today believes the word 'sin' to encourage. And nothing could be more remote from our minds if we insist on thinking of sin as yummy transgression or titillating naughtiness, and evil as the inexcusable and irredeemable faults of monstrous others.

In this exploration we have travelled from Evagrius' eight thoughts to six clusters of two dozen vices and identified various types of temptation. Finally, we have identified seven tactics to help us with the demon wrestling that is an inevitable and ongoing part of every human life that is not destined for the inferno. Not that there is any such place as Dante or countless others have envisioned and imagined. Hell is the loneliness of the self that comes when we succumb to the hostility of pleasures that would isolate us in vice. Like virtue, vice is its own reward, locking us inside the claustrophobic box where time hangs with infinite heaviness and the hostility of our ill-chosen pleasures, our frustrated attempts to control, and our fury at not being the subject of the admiring attention of others dominates our every endless moment.

The wisest, and happiest thing for us to do as human beings is to take steps to avoid getting trapped in such a living hell. The seven tactics set out here are intended to offer a way forward, whatever the starting point, that is based on such an understanding of the dark side of the soul and the web of sin as has been developed by meditating on the six clusters of vice identified in the central chapters of this book. The pathway involves recognizing that sin is a serious spiritual issue, developing some spiritual assertiveness, learning from others, seeking humility, setting time-wise goals, learning to love and identifying what is not love-worthy. And it is one to be embarked upon positively, and in a spirit of hope.

Sin, as Julian of Norwich put it, is 'behovely'. Like 'acedia', this word is no longer part of our English vocabulary. 'Behovely' means something like 'necessary'. There is no life without sin; certainly no person or process or community without sin. 'If we say we have no sin we deceive ourselves' is how St John puts it in one of his letters. To think about sin, to dwell on it, to meditate about its complexities and problems, is not to engage in a blame-game or to wallow self-indulgently in shame, but to explore the human condition from the murky inside in the interests of personal flourishing and the common good.

'Sin is behovely', wrote Mother Julian the hermit. It is necessary, inevitable. That wasn't the end of her sentence any more than the analysis of the six clusters of sin was the end of this book. We can't live without sin, and we can't imagine any kind of community without vicious vice. But that's not the end of the story, by any means.

'Sin is behovely, but all shall be well and all shall be well and all manner of thing shall be well.' *That* is the end of the story. With faith like this we might dare to take a flickering candle into the dark side of our soul and calmly begin to unpick the web of sin in which, if we are wise, we will find ourselves before we are utterly entangled.

NOTES

The following notes may be of interest to those who are intrigued to know what lies behind my assertions and opinions. Full details of each publication that is quoted are given the first time it is mentioned.

Prologue – The Viciousness of Vice

It is Derek Nelson who seeks to reconcile individualistic and social approaches to sin by insisting that the self is relational in *What's Wrong with Sin: Sin in Individual and Social Perspective from Schleiermacher to Theologies of Liberation*, London, Continuum, 2009.

Gabriele Taylor talks about the viciousness of the vices on page 30 of her *Deadly Vices*, Oxford, Clarendon Press, 2006.

The quotation from Chaucer's *Canterbury Tales* is taken from page 178 of Shaun Tucker's helpful compendium *The Virtues and Vices in the Arts: A Sourcebook*, Eugene, OR, Cascade Books, 2015. Taylor is here quoting J.W. Nicholson's modernized version (Garden City, N.Y., International Collection Library, 1974). The original is: 'Ful ofte tyme I rede that no man truste in his owene perfeccioun, but he be stronger than Sampson, and hoolier than David, and wiser than Salomon.'

Chapter 1: The Dark Side of the Soul

Page 5 **Studying Sin** – Alistair McFadyen makes these remarks on the opening page (p. 3) of his *Bound to Sin: Abuse, Holocaust and the Christian Doctrine of Sin*, Cambridge, Cambridge University Press, 2000.

'The wages of sin is death' (Romans 6.23). All biblical quotations in this book, unless it is otherwise mentioned, are from the New Revised Standard Version (NRSV).

Francis Spufford has a chapter on sin in *Unapologetic*, London, Faber & Faber, 2013. The quotation is from page 26.

Page 9   **Naming Evil** – David Cameron's remarks were widely reported in the media.

Page 13   **As a Bee Produces Honey** – As well as basing *Lord of the Flies* on his understanding of original sin, Golding explored the notion in the much less well-known novel about the primordial meeting of the Neanderthals with *Homo sapiens*: *The Inheritors*. The quote is from pages 260–261 of John Carey, *William Golding: The Man who Wrote Lord of the Flies*, London, Faber & Faber, 2009.

The Stanford Prison Experiment is written up in Philip Zimbardo's book *The Lucifer Effect: Understanding How Good People Turn Evil*, New York, Random House, 2007. It is now the subject of a Hollywood film. Stanley Milgram's work is well known but was originally published as a paper entitled 'The Behavioral Study of Obedience' in *The Journal of Abnormal and Social Psychology* 67(4), 1963.

St Paul wrote about not doing what he intended to do in Romans 7.14–24. The passage that I have adapted should also be noted in its undoctored form.

> For we know that the law is spiritual; but I am of the flesh, sold into slavery under sin. I do not understand my own actions. For I do not do what I want, but I do the very thing I hate. Now if I do what I do not want, I agree that the law is good. But in fact it is no longer I that do it, but sin that dwells within me. For I know that nothing good dwells within me, that is, in my flesh. I can will what is right, but I cannot do it. For I do not do the good I want, but the evil I do not want is what I do. Now if I do what I do not want, it is no longer I that do it, but sin that dwells within me.
>
> So I find it to be a law that when I want to do what is good, evil lies close at hand. For I delight in the law of God in my inmost self, but I see in my members another law at war with the law of my mind, making me captive to the law of sin that dwells in my members. Wretched man that I am! Who will rescue me from this body of death?

Page 17   **Murky Border County** – Simon Laham, *The Joy of Sin*, London, Constable, 2012.

Christopher Cook suggests the phrase 'hostile pleasures' on page 98 of his book *The Philokalia and the Inner Life: On Passions and Prayer*, Cambridge, James Clarke and Co., 2011. Cook goes on to write, 'In a dynamic process, which invites comparison with the phenomenon of addiction, they confer both pleasure and pain, they attract and enslave, they seduce and destroy'.

The long quotation from Alexander Solzhenitsyn is from page 312 of *The Gulag Archipelago*, translated from the Russian by Thomas P. Whitney and Harry Willets, and abridged by Edward E. Ericson, Jr, London, The Harvill Press, 1985.

'All have sinned . . ' (Romans 3.23).

'Judge not . . ' (Luke 6.37). King James Version.

'Why do you see . . ' (Luke 6.41–42).

Chapter 2: The Deadlies

Page 24 **A Little List** – The word 'acedia' is pronounced 'ay-seed-ee-ah'.

Rainer E. Jehl compares acedia with burnout syndrome in an essay in the book edited by Richard Newhauser, *The Garden of Evil: The Vices and Culture in the Middle Ages*, Toronto, Pontifical Institute of Medieval Studies, 2005.

The following works explore and explain Evagrius of Pontus: Christopher C. H. Cook. *The Philokalia and the Inner Life: On Passions and Prayer*, Cambridge, James Clarke & Co., 2011; Robert E. Sinkewicz, *Evagrius of Pontus: The Greek Ascetic Corpus*, Oxford, Oxford University Press, 2003; Angela Tilby, *The Seven Deadly Sins: Their Origin in the Spiritual Teaching of Evagrius the Hermit*, London, SPCK, 2009.

See page 86 of Tucker, *The Virtues and Vices in the Arts*.

Page 28 **From Thoughts to Vices** – John Bossy makes the point about the Ten Commandments superseding the seven deadly sins on page 38 of *Christianity in the West 1400–1700*, Oxford, Oxford University Press, 1985.

Gabriele Taylor asserts the rightness of the 'seven deadly sins' on the first page of *Deadly Vices*.

Judith Shklar explains Montaigne's concept of ordinary vices in the introduction to her *Ordinary Vices*, Cambridge, MA, The Belknap Press, 1984.

Page 32   **Not Quite So Simple** – Laham's assertion that 'even the deadliest of vices can make you smart' is from page vii and the two longer quotes are from page 201 of *The Joy of Sin*.

I have learnt about the seven deadly sins and children's literature (and film) from websites such as the following: https://www.reddit.com /r/FanTheories/comments/2aay9f/winnie_the_pooh_and_the_seven_ deadly_sins/; http://hypervocal.com/entertainment/2012/wonka-7- deadly-sins/.

Mary Midgley's words about 'complex states' is from page 3 of her book *Wickedness*, London, Routledge & Kegan Paul, 1984.

Chapter 3: Naughty, But Nice

The quote from Francis Spufford is an extended version of the quote already cited from his book *Unapologetic*.

Page 38   **Gluttony** – The passage in which Jesus expresses a liberal attitude towards food is from Mark 7.18–23.

'Take, eat . . .' This phrase is from the biblical passage known as the Institution of the Lord's Supper as recorded in Matthew 26.26–30. Parallel but slightly different versions are found in Mark 14.22–25, Luke 22.14–23 and 1 Corinthians 11.23–26.

Dante locates the gluttonous near the top of purgatory, on the sixth cornice, just below the promiscuous and above the avaricious. They are not only lean and hungry, but tormented by the scent of an apple they cannot reach to eat.

See *The Joy of Sin*, chapter 2. In it Laham reports a psychological experiment that he believes supports his view that there is nothing sinful about eating to excess, in part because we are socialized to 'clear the plate'. This cunning experiment involves inviting the subjects to drink as much soup as they like. The one group have normal bowls which are refilled on demand from a generous supply by the familiar method of ladle and saucepan. The other group have self-filling bowls that are connected by a tube to a hidden reservoir of soup. The second group consistently take more soup – being motivated, though tragically never able, to clear their plates. Laham reports these experiments by Brian Wansink on pages 32–34.

Locating gluttony in fussiness does not originate with Aquinas but goes back to Evagrius, for whom gluttony, avarice and vainglory were the fundamental 'thoughts'. 'All the other demons', he wrote, 'march along behind these ones and in their turn take up with the people wounded by these.' Sinkewicz, *Evagrius of Pontus*, page 153.

Fat is a Feminist Issue was written by Suzie Orbach and the first edition was published in 1978.

Page 44 **Intoxication** – Our anthropologist is Professor Alan Macfarlane, who discusses 'mildly intoxicating substances' on pages 216–20 of *Reflections on Cambridge*, New Delhi, Social Science Press, 2009.

In 2009, Professor David Nutt was sacked by the then Home Secretary from his post as chairman of ACDM (The Association of Clinical Data Management) for publicly reiterating his view that cannabis is less harmful than alcohol.

The chapter by Alan Howarth entitled 'Drugs: Harm Reduction' has been particularly helpful in preparing this chapter and many of the facts quoted are taken from there. Lord Howarth served first as a Conservative and then as a Labour MP. At the time of writing his chapter (which was first given as a lecture) he was an officer of the All Party Parliamentary Group for Drug Policy Reform. The chapter is in Christopher Clarke, *The Too Difficult Box: The Big Issues Politicians Can't Crack*, London, Biteback Publishing, 2014.

Islam is famously a teetotal religion, and the Salvation Army is a form of Christianity that prohibits the use of alcohol. The Church of Jesus Christ of Latter-day Saints prohibits not only alcohol and tobacco but also caffeine.

The Methodist Church does not allow the consumption of alcohol on its premises, even in the form of communion wine (unless the premises are being used by another denomination for a communion service). It is a church that has given more reflection than most to the question of alcohol use, which is why it is worth considering its position in some detail. The 1987 position has not been superseded and is included in the current edition of *The Constitutional Practice and Discipline of the Methodist Church*, http://www.methodist.org.uk/media/633296/cpd-vol-2-0913.pdf.

Although 'Snakes and Ladders' is a game with Hindu origins the Victorians appropriated it to the cause of moral education, so that in some versions the snakes were labelled with the deadly sins and the ladders with the contrary virtues.

Page 52 **Talkativeness** – *Hamartiology* is 'the study of sin' and so 'hamartiological texts' are books, sermon, treaties etc. about sin. The word 'hamartia' is a Greek word deriving from the word for archery and literally means 'missing the target'.

Butler's sermon was preached at the Rolls Chapel and published first in 1726. It was most recently published in *Butler's Fifteen Sermons Preached at the Rolls Chapel and A Dissertation of the Nature of Virtue* by Joseph Butler, London, SPCK, 1970.

'If any man among you . . .' (James 1.26). King James Version.

'. . . a time to keep silence and a time to speak'. (Ecclesiastes 3.7) (Butler reverses the biblical order of silence and speech in his sermon.)

TED (Technology, Entertainment, Design) – Conferences are held in various centres, the talks are posted online; some attract huge seven figure audiences for their 'ideas worth spreading'. See Carmine Gallo, *Talk Like Ted*; The *9 Public-Speaking Secrets of the World's Top Minds*, New York, St. Martin's Griffin, 2014.

The case of Sally Bercow and Lord McAlpine was widely reported in the media when the out-of-court settlement was made in October 2013.

The book alluded to is *Quiet: The Power of Introverts in a World that Can't Stop Talking*, by Susan Cain. See also her TED talk, 'The Power of Introverts'; https://www.ted.com/talks/susan_cain_the_power_of_introverts.

Chapter 4: Vicious Regards

Page 59 **Snobbery** – Judith Shklar considers snobbery in *Ordinary Vices*, chapter 3, pp. 87–137. The footnote I mention is on page 254.

William Makepeace Thackeray's *Book of Snobs* is available online at http://www.gutenberg.org/files/2686/2686-h/2686-h.htm.

Wendell Berry considers 'historical self-righteousness' in his essay *Writer and Region*. The quotes are from page 81 of his collection *What Are People For?* Berkeley, Counterpoint, 2010.

Page 67 **Vanity** – The subject of fame is also discussed here under the heading of 'boredom' in chapter 6.

Taylor is writing in *Deadly Vices*, page 73.

Jesus' temptation to throw himself from the Temple is one of three experienced in the wilderness. The other two were to turn stones into bread and to bow down and worship Satan. See Matthew 4.1–11.

Jesus' teaching about your left hand not knowing what your right hand is doing when it comes to giving alms is in the Sermon on the Mount (Matthew 6.3). Although the phrase has become a proverb for poor organization and administration, when Jesus used it he was speaking of a positive aspiration.

The second Taylor quote in this chapter is from page 71 of *Deadly Vices*.

Thinking of vanity and vainglory as entry-level vices raises the question of where they lead. One suggestion is 'perfectionism', which I consider in chapter 5. The connections with narcissism, which I consider under that heading, are plain.

Page 74   **Pride** – I write about both good pride and pride in chapter 4 of *Barefoot Disciple: Walking the Way of Passionate Humility*, London, Continuum, 2010.

In his famous poem *If*, Rudyard Kipling writes,

> If you can meet with Triumph and Disaster
> And treat those two impostors just the same . . .

The famous comment 'hell is other people' comes from Sartre's play *Huis Clos*. Although I have used it for its commonly understood meaning – i.e. an exaggerated sense of the irksomeness of others – the meaning in context is more like the definition of hell that I propose, referring to the hell of being the depersonalized object of another's relentless gaze.

Gabriele Taylor talks of the esteem-worthy self on page 82 of *Deadly Vices*.

Manfred F. R. Kets de Vries' book is *Lessons on Leadership by Terror: Finding Shaka Zulu in the Attic*, Cheltenham, UK, Edward Elgar, 2004.

Page 80   **Abjectness** – Iris Murdoch makes this point in her essay on humility in *The Sovereignty of Good*, London, Routledge & Kegan Paul, 1970.

Page 87   **Envy** – Gurcharan Das discusses envy in chapter 2 of *The Difficulty of Being Good: On the Subtle Art of Dharma*, London, Allen Lane, 2009.

Jacob Epstein, *Envy*, Oxford, Oxford University Press, 2003.

Chapter 5: Impossible Ideals

The long quotation about integrity is taken from this webpage: http://www.goal-setting-guide.com/the-importance-of-integrity/.

The little prayer of St Augustine is a popular version of a slightly more nuanced one that appears in book 8 of *Confessions*. Here the quotation is embedded in its context, which makes it clear that Augustine now deplores the attitude that it reflects. Nonetheless, it is a genuine insight into the reality of human beings. The translation here is that of Henry Chadwick, Oxford University Press, 1991, page 145.

> But I was an unhappy young man, wretched as at the beginning of my adolescence when I prayed you for chastity and said: 'Grant me chastity and continence, but not yet.' I was afraid you might hear my prayer quickly, and that you might too rapidly heal me of the disease of lust which I preferred to satisfy rather than suppress. I had gone along 'evil ways' (Ecclus. 2: 10) with a sacrilegious superstition, not indeed because I felt sure of its truth but because I preferred it to the alternatives, which I did not investigate in a devout spirit but opposed in an attitude of hostility.

Page 97 **Hypocrisy** – The quotes from the Bible are from the Sermon on the Mount in Matthew 6.5 and 16, respectively.

Jesus responds, in Matthew 15.1–9, to the accusation that his disciples do not wash their hands.

Evidence that praise can have negative consequences can be found in the work of Carol S. Dweck. See for instance her article, 'The Perils and Promises of Praise' in *Educational Leadership* 65 (2) (October 2007), pages 34–39, where she claims that her research shows that the widely held belief that praising students' intelligence builds their confidence and motivation to learn is false.

Judith Shklar discusses hypocrisy in the second chapter of *Ordinary Vices*. All the quotes here are from pages 54 and 55.

Page 108 **Defensiveness** – 'the truth will make you free' (John 8.32).

On narcissism see the work of Jean Twenge and others, in particular *The Narcissism Epidemic: Living in the Age of Entitlement*, New York, Free Press, 2009. I also discussed narcissism in chapter 4 in the context of vanity and return to it later in this chapter in the context of perfectionism.

Page 113 **Certainty** – Mary Midgley discusses these matters in chapter 3 of *Wickedness*. The quotes are from page 60.

The Solzhenitsyn quote is as above.

Page 118 **Perfectionism** – Jesus said 'Be ye ... perfect' in the Sermon on the Mount in Matthew 5.48. He said, 'seek ye first the kingdom of God' in Matthew 6.33. These are words from the King James Version.

The cited research on narcissism is in an academic paper by Patricia M. Greenfield, of the Department of Psychology at the University of California in Los Angeles. 'The Changing Psychology of Culture From 1800 Through 2000' was published in *Psychological Science* 24(9) (September 2013), 1722–31. More academic articles on the rise of narcissism are listed here: https://www.psychologytoday.com/blog/the-narcissism-epidemic/201308/how-dare-you-say-narcissism-is-increasing (accessed 25 August 2015).

Narcissism is recognized as a personality disorder in the *Diagnostic and Statistical Manual of Mental Disorders*, fifth edition (DSM-5), which is the standard classification of mental disorders used by mental health professionals in the United States.

Bruno Bettelheim's *A Good Enough Parent* was published in 1987. Bettelheim was born in Vienna in 1903 and spent twelve months in concentration camps during the Nazi era. This had a profound effect on him as a person and psychologist, and he went on to found the Orthogenic School at the University of Chicago, working with and healing highly disturbed children – those 'nobody could stand'.

Chapter 6: Temporal Dislocations

Page 125 **Introduction** – As well as important ancient resources about acedia there are a number of recent books that explore the subject, among them Kathleen Norris' personal and accessible *New York Times* bestseller, *Acedia and Me: A Marriage, Monks and A Writer's Life*, New York, Riverhead Books, 2008. See also R. J. Snell, *Acedia and Its Discontents: Metaphysical Boredom in an Empire of Desire*, Kettering, OH, Angelico Press. The most comprehensive view of the way acedia was regarded in the Middle Ages is Siegfried Wenzel, *The Sins of Sloth: Acedia in Medieval Thought and Literature*, Durham, NC, The University of North Carolina Press, 1960.

The quotes from Kathleen Norris' *Acedia and Me* are from pages 6 and 231.

Page 129 **Sloth** – Wendy Wasserstein's book is simply called *Sloth*. In it, as the cover blurb says, she both 'pokes fun at the self-help industry and satirizes the legion of Americans who are cultural and political sloths'. Wendy Wasserstein, *Sloth*, Oxford, Oxford University Press, 2005.

Laham gives a whole chapter to sloth, as he does to the other traditional deadly sins.

The 'Iron Rule' was coined by Saul Alinsky. See Edward T. Chambers, *Roots for Radicals: Organizing for Power, Action, and Justice*, New York, Continuum, 2003.

The Mary Midgley quote is from page 133 of *Wickedness*.

Page 135 **Boredom** – The quote from Evagrius comes from his work called *Praktikos*. See Robert Sinkewicz, *Evagrius of Pontus*, page 99.

The quote about time becoming 'refractory' comes from page 128 of Lars A. Svendsen, *Philosophy of Boredom*, translated by John Irons, London, Reaktion Books, 2005. He makes the point about boredom being a 'non-mood' on page 129. Svendsen has an extended discussion of Warhol and boredom on pages 100–106, a subject we visited when considering vanity and vainglory in chapter 4.

There is an extended analysis of 'situational' boredom in Peter Toohey, *Boredom: A Lively History*, New Haven and London, Yale University Press, 2011. The author makes several connections with the emotion of disgust and suggests the aptness of the expression 'fed up'.

Page 140 **Busyness** – I write about 'white-rabbit behaviour' and how to deal with it by developing 'time wisdom' in two books: Stephen Cherry, *Beyond Busyness: Time Wisdom for Ministry*, Durham, Sacristy Press, 2012; Stephen Cherry, *Beyond Busyness: Time Wisdom in an Hour*, Durham, Sacristy Press, 2013.

The contemplative couplet is the first two lines of William Henry Davies' poem, *Leisure*.

The research on various 'time traps' is reported in the fourth edition of the time-management book by Alec Mackenzie and Pat Nickerson, *The Time Trap*, New York, AMACOM, 2009.

Page 145 **Nostalgia** – Claudia Hammond explains the 'reminiscence bump' on pages 185–90 of her book *Time Warped*, Edinburgh, Canongate, 2012.

A website that supports Eckhart Tolle's book *The Power of Now* makes various claims for the power of focusing on the present moment: https://www.eckharttolle.com/article/The-Power-Of-Now-Spirituality-And-The-End-Of-Suffering.

Philip Zimbardo and John Boyd, *The Time Paradox: The New Psychology of Time*, London, Rider, 2008. This book also has a connected website – http://www.thetimeparadox.com – which incorporates a link to the 'Zimbardo Time Perspective Inventory' (ZTPI).

Chapter 7: Tragic Desires

Page 152 Lust – I refer to Marie Keenan's book, *Child Sexual Abuse and the Roman Catholic Church: Gender, Power, and Organizational Culture*, Oxford, Oxford University Press, 2012. I quote from pages 15, 39 and 247.

Evagrius' aphorism about a poisoned arrow is from his *Eight Thoughts*, as translated by Robert Sinkewicz – page 76 of *Evagrius of Pontus*.

'Who told thee . . .' (Genesis 3.11). King James Version.

Laham's chapter on lust is the first in *The Joy of Sin*.

Mihaly Csikszentmihalyi discusses sex in chapter 5, 'The Body in Flow', of *Flow: The Classic Work on How to Achieve Happiness*, London, Rider, 1992; reissued with a new introduction, 2002.

Jesus' comment on adultery is from Matthew 5.27–28.

Page 159 Greed – '. . . the love of money . . .' is found in 1 Timothy 6.10.

'. . . high heaven rejects the lore / Of nicely-calculated less or more' is from Wordsworth's Ecclesiastical Sonnet 'Inside of King's College Chapel'.

The story of Ananias and Sapphira is in Acts 5.1–11.

'Render therefore unto Caesar . . .' (Matthew 22.21 and Mark 12.17). King James Version

'No one can serve God and mammon . . .' (Matthew 6.24 and Luke 16.13). King James Version.

Abraham Cowley's essay 'Of Avarice' is collected in *The Essays and Other Prose Writings*, ed. Alfred B. Gough Oxford, Clarendon Press, 1915. The quotations used are from pages 189–91.

The film *Wall Street* was directed by Oliver Stone and released in 1987. The screenplay was by Oliver Stone and Stanley Weiser. The passage quoted was transcribed from the screenplay.

Page 166 **Insatiability** – The various quotations from the Skidelskys here are from chapter 1, 'Keynes's Mistake', of Robert Skidelsky and Edward Skidelsky, *How Much Is Enough? The Love of Money and the Case for the Good Life*, London, Allen Lane, 2012.

Positional or 'oligarchic' goods are often contrasted with democratic goods. These are goods that, in theory at least, can be enjoyed by many.

Page 172 **Control** – Lady Catherine de Bourgh meets Elizabeth Bennet in chapter 56 – that is, 14 of volume 3 – of *Pride and Prejudice*.

Jim Collins discusses Level 5 Leadership in chapter 2 of *Good to Great: Why Some Companies Make the Leap . . . and Others Don't*, London, Random House, 2001.

Whether or not one buys McGilchrist's conclusions is a decision that should be made on the basis not of reading these few paragraphs but of working through his four-hundred-page argument which is set out in remarkably tiny print, and the almost one hundred pages of academic apparatus that follow – in an even smaller typeface. Iain McGilchrist, *The Master and His Emissary: The Divided Brain and the Making of the Western World*, London, Yale University Press, 2010.

McGilchrist talks about the inversion of Scheler's pyramid of values on page 160, the end of the Roman Empire on page 297, and the power-hungry on page 319.

Chapter 8: Malicious Tendencies

I wrote up my experiences in the aftermath of the murder of Adam Morrell, the teenage boy who was tortured and then put to death by a gang to which he had attached himself, in a chapter called 'Representation' in Samuel Wells and Sarah Coakley, *Praying for England*, London, Continuum, 2012.

Page 180 Cruelty – Judith Shklar discusses cruelty extensively in chapter 1 of *Ordinary Vices*. She writes about cruelty disfiguring human character on page 9.

Aviad Kleinberg describes his destruction of Micky's city on pages 4 and 5 of *Seven Deadly Sins: A Very Partial List*, trans. Susan Emanuel in collaboration with the author, Cambridge, MA, The Belknap Press, 2008.

Page 185 Rage – The killing of Mr Don Lock took place in July 2015, and was widely reported in the media.

The story of Moses returning to the idolatrous Israelites with the Ten Commandments in Exodus 32.19–20 shows the anger of Moses being kindled: 'As soon as he came near the camp and saw the calf and the dancing, Moses' anger burned hot, and he threw the tablets from his hands and broke them at the foot of the mountain. He took the calf that they had made, burned it with fire, ground it to powder, scattered it on the water, and made the Israelites drink it.'

Psalm 78 is a long narrative poem that tells the story of the relationship between God and God's people. The quotation is from verses 60 and 66, a passage where the wrath of God is vividly portrayed. The translation is that of Miles Coverdale which is used in the *Book of Common Prayer*.

> When God heard this, he was wroth: and took sore displeasure at Israel. So that he forsook the tabernacle in Silo: even the tent that he had pitched among men. He delivered their power into captivity: and their beauty into the enemy's hand. He gave his people over also unto the sword: and was wroth with his inheritance. The fire consumed their young men: and their maidens were not given to marriage. Their priests were slain with the sword: and there were no widows to make lamentation. So the Lord awaked as one out of sleep: and like a giant refreshed with wine. He smote his enemies in the hinder parts: and put them to a perpetual shame.

Jesus cleanses the Temple in Matthew 21.12–17 and John 2.12–22.

The passage I am referring to in Galatians is where Paul is angry with those who are insisting on the circumcision of gentile converts – Galatians 5.11–12: 'But my friends, why am I still being persecuted if I am still preaching circumcision? In that case the offence of the cross has been removed. I wish those who unsettle you would castrate themselves!'

The first quote from Evagrius is from *Eight Thoughts* as translated by Robert Sinkewicz in *Evagrius of Pontus*, p. 80. Evagrius records twenty-one aphorisms about anger, of which this is the first. The second is from the work known as *The Monk: A Treatise on the Practical Life*, often known as *Prakitikos*. Again, this is Sinkewicz's translation, p. 99.

The quote from Mary Midgley is from page 68 of *Wickedness*.

Page 191 **Revenge** – I make use here of Trudy Govier's analysis of revenge in her *Forgiveness and Revenge*, London, Routledge, 2002. The quotes are from pages 2 and 12 respectively and in both cases the emphasis is in the original.

Chapter 9: The Web of Sin

Page 199 **Sin Suits its Times** – There are two quotations here from Paula Fredriksen's scholarly book about the theology of sin as it evolved in the first five centuries of the Christian era – *Sin: The Early History of an Idea*, Princeton, NJ, Princeton University Press, 2012. The first is from page 150. The words that I have used as the subtitle of this part of the chapter are the very final ones of the book. The other quotations are from page 147.

Mary Midgley discusses Satan's qualities on page 137 of *Wickedness*.

Chapter 10: Demon Wrestling: A Practical Guide

Page 215 **Types of Temptation** – C. S. Lewis' *The Screwtape Letters* have been published many times in many formats, so rather than give page numbers I will identify the specific letter from which each quotation comes. They are, respectively, as follows: 1, 6, 8, 8, 15. Lewis uses masculine pronouns and refers to men throughout.

Page 221 **Answering Back** – I have used the edition translated by David Brakke of Evagrius' *Antirrheticus*: *Evagrius of Pontus, Talking Back: A Monastic Handbook for Combating Demons*, Collegeville, MI, The Liturgical

Press, 2009. The passages on love of money are from pages 85–99, and the biblical verses quoted are Deuteronomy 15.7–8, Deuteronomy 28.17–18, Psalm 44.11–12, Matthew 6.19 and Ephesians 4.32. Those on anger are from pages 119–32, and the biblical verses quoted are Exodus 23.7, Proverbs 12.16, Proverbs 15.1 and Proverbs 15.8. The quotation regarding vainglory is from pages 156–7 and the biblical passage quoted is James 3.1–2. The biblical verses are not from the NRSV.

Page 225 **Seven Tactics for Demon Wrestling** – In his book *Pope Francis: Untying the Knots*, London, Bloomsbury, 2013, Paul Vallely has outlined his understanding of the way in which Pope Francis has discovered the importance of humility and sought to learn and demonstrate it. The particular quote here is from an article in *The Atlantic*, 23 August 2015, 'How Pope Francis Learned Humility'.

Epilogue – All Shall Be Well

The first, long quote from Kathleen Norris is from *Acedia and Me*, pages 169–70. The second is from page 281.

The quote from Iain McGilchrist's *The Master and His Emissary* is from page 323.

The phrase 'yummy temptation' is not mine, alas, but Francis Spufford's – see *Unapologetic*.

'If we say we have no sin . . .' is from 1 John 1.8.

The famous quote from the *Shewings* of Julian of Norwich deserves to be rendered in full in the original Middle English.

> And after this, oure lorde brought to my minde the longing that I had to him before. And I saw that nothing letted [hindered] me but sinne. And so I behelde generally in us alle, and methought: 'If sinne had not be, we shulde all have be clene and like to oure lorde as he made us.' And thus in my foly before this time, often I wondred why, by the grete forseeing wisdom of God, the beginning of sinne was not letted [prevented]. For then thought me that alle shulde have be wele.
>   This sterling [thought] was mekille [greatly] to be forsaken [mistaken], and neverthelesse morning and sorrow I made

therefore without reson and discretion. But Jhesu, that in this vision enformed me of all that me neded, answered by his worde and saide: "Sinne is behovely [necessary], but alle shalle be wele, and alle shalle be wele, and alle manner of thinge shalle be wel."

The Writings of Julian of Norwich, edited by Nicholas Watson and Jacqueline Jenkins, Turnhout, Belgium, Brepols Publishers, 2006. p206/7. This extract is from the twenty seventh chapter of 'The Revelation of Love' which describes the thirteenth revelation.

ACKNOWLEDGEMENTS

This book has its origins in a chance conversation had with Alastair Redfern, Bishop of Derby, in the nave of Durham Cathedral one sunny Saturday morning in September 2012. We were talking about my book on forgiveness, and he suggested that 'sin' was another subject that was just off the horizon and waiting for a fresh look. Later that day I had sketched out my first thoughts for such a volume.

Not that they were much good. And that is why it is a whole three years later and in a city that has no cathedral, that the book at last comes to be finished, one sunny day in October. It has been a long journey and I have spoken with many people, individuals and groups, in many different settings, about the themes and issues discussed here. I am grateful to kind listeners, and especially to those who offered comments and further reflections. Speaking and indeed preaching about sins, especially deadly ones, seems to strike a chord. And this resonance encouraged me to persist with work on the book despite the wry looks that people inevitably gave me when I told them I was focusing on sin these days, and the upheaval to moving to a new post in another part of the country.

I had hoped, as many might imagine, that the manuscripts of the various talks and sermons I gave would provide ready-made chapters or sections of this book. This has hardly been the case, due largely to the way in which I have found it necessary to re-think these issues, and indeed the structure of the book, so many times. Nonetheless,

I should confess that the section on envy started life as a sermon in a series on the seven deadly sins at the Chapel of Hatfield College, Durham and that the section on talkativeness started out as a sermon at Matins at Durham Cathedral, where the preacher faces the stone tablet that memorializes Bishop Joseph Butler, whose own eighteenth-century sermon on the same subject I was exploring. This made me realize that while one can't expect to say much that is new about sin, it is important to try to keep talking carefully about it and to connect it with the issues of the day and the concerns that press on people's hearts and minds.

My biggest debt is to those who have thought about, and written about, this subject in the past, together with those who have been kind enough either to listen to me trying to be articulate about it, or to have been gracious enough to want to take the exchange further. Various friends have been vigilant in their spiritual support for the duration. For this I am especially grateful, as the challenges with this subject are manifold and multi-dimensional. I am also very grateful to Caroline Chartres and her colleagues at Bloomsbury, whose patience through a gestation period that was far more protracted than we anticipated has been exemplary. And to Maggie, who, as ever, has encouraged me to stick at it, and has been generously accommodating as the work has impacted on domestic life.

INDEX